The Icons of the Wild West: Wyatt Earp, Doc Holliday, Wild Bill Hickok, Jesse James, Billy the Kid and Butch Cassidy

By Charles River Editors

About Charles River Editors

Charles River Editors was founded by Harvard and MIT alumni to provide superior editing and original writing services, with the expertise to create digital content for publishers across a vast range of subject matter. In addition to providing original digital content for third party publishers, Charles River Editors republishes civilization's greatest literary works, bringing them to a new generation via ebooks.

Introduction

Wild Bill Hickok (1837-1876)

"Wild Bill was a strange character. Add to this figure a costume blending the immaculate neatness of the dandy with the extravagant taste and style of a frontiersman, you have Wild Bill, the most famous scout on the Plains."" – General George Custer

Separating fact from fiction when it comes to the life of Wild Bill is nearly impossible, something due in great measure to the fact that the man himself exaggerated his own adventures or fabricated stories altogether. When he was killed while playing poker in the mining South Dakotan outpost of Deadwood, he put Deadwood on the map and ensured both his place and his poker hand's place in legend.

The best known aspects of Hickok's life hardly distinguish him from other famous Westerners. Like so many others, Hickok headed west as a fugitive of justice, yet that didn't prevent him from becoming a frontier lawman in Kansas, like Wyatt Earp. Hickok also became well known in the West for being a professional gambler and a remarkably quick draw who proved quite deadly in shootouts, like Doc Holliday.

What made Hickok stand out from so many of his day was that he was both successful at what he did and he managed to cultivate his own legend through tales of his exploits. By the mid-

1870s, Hickok was notorious enough that he went out of his way to play cards with his back to the wall so he could see anyone approaching him. On one of the few occasions he did not, August 2, 1876, he was shot in the back of the head by Jack McCall while holding two pair, Aces and Eights (all black), now known as the Dead Man's Hand.

Whether Hickok's legacy would have endured without his legendary death is anyone's guess, but by becoming the first well known Westerner to die with his boots on, he immediately became the West's first hero. Hickok and his life story became the subject of countless "dime store" novels which cast him in larger than life roles loosely based on his adventures or entirely made up. Once Wild Bill became a fixture of American pop culture, he stayed there, and he continues to be depicted in television, movies, and the like.

The Icons of the Wild West chronicles Wild Bill's life, while also analyzing his legacy and the mythology that has enveloped his story, attempting to separate fact from fiction to determine what the frontier legend was really like. Along with pictures of important people, places, and events in his life, you will learn about Wild Bill like you never have before, in no time at all.

Wyatt Earp (1848-1929)

"For my handling of the situation at Tombstone, I have no regrets. Were it to be done over again, I would do exactly as I did at that time. If the outlaws and their friends and allies imagined that they could intimidate or exterminate the Earps by a process of assassination, and then hide behind alibis and the technicalities of the law, they simply missed their guess." – Wyatt Earp

Of all the colorful characters that inhabited the West during the 19th century, the most famous of them all is Wyatt Earp (1848-1929), who has long been regarded as the embodiment of the Wild West. Considered the "toughest and deadliest gunman of his day", Earp symbolized the swagger, the heroism, and even the lawlessness of the West, notorious for being a law enforcer, gambler, saloon keeper, and vigilante. The Western icon is best known for being a sheriff in Tombstone, but before that he had been arrested and jailed several times himself, in one case escaping from prison, and he was not above gambling and spending time in "houses of ill-fame".

The seminal moment in Earp's life also happened to be the West's most famous gunfight, the Gunfight at the O.K. Corral, which famously pitted Earp, his brothers Morgan and Virgil, and Doc Holliday against Billy Clanton, Tom McLaury and Frank McLaury. Though the gunfight lasted less than a minute, it is still widely remembered as the climactic event of the period, representing lawlessness and justice, vendettas, and a uniquely Western moral code. For Earp, the aftermath led to assassination attempts on his brothers, one of which was successful, touching off the "Earp Vendetta Ride".

By the end of the 19th century, Earp was already a poignant symbol of that time and day, having permanently etched his name in the folklore of the West, but he stayed out west, engaging in everything from gold mining to vigilante justice on the Mexican border. A living legend, he even served as an advisor to early Hollywood, which was already pumping out Western movies. When he died in 1929 at the age of 80, one of the West's toughest fighers and one of its longest survivors had finally passed

The Icons of the Wild West details Earp's amazing life and career, including all of its famous ups and infamous downs, while also analyzing his legacy and the mythology that has enveloped his story. Along with pictures of important people, places, and events in his life, you will learn about Wyatt Earp like you never have before, in no time at all.

John Henry "Doc" Holliday (1851-1887)

"Doc was a dentist, not a lawman or an assassin, whom necessity had made a gambler; a gentleman whom disease had made a frontier vagabond; a philosopher whom life had made a caustic wit; a long lean ash-blond fellow nearly dead with consumption, and at the same time the most skillful gambler and the nerviest, speediest, deadliest man with a six-gun that I ever knew."
– Wyatt Earp

Of all the colorful characters that inhabited the West during the 19th century, the man who has earned an enduring legacy as the region's quirkiest is John Henry "Doc" Holliday (1851-1887), a dentist turned professional gambler who was widely recognized as one of the fastest draws in the West. In fact, the only thing that might have been faster than the deadly gunman's draw was his violent temper, which was easily set off when Holliday was drunk. By the early 1880s, Holliday had been arrested nearly 20 times.

That said, there were plenty of men in the West who gambled, drank, and dueled, and Holliday may have been lumped in with those whose names were forgotten but for his association with Wyatt Earp. It was this friendship that led to Holliday's role in the West's most famous shootout, the Gunfight at the O.K. Corrall, as well as the Earp Vendetta Ride. For those two events alone, Holliday's legacy has endured, and his unique characteristics have added a mystique, legendary quality to it.

Next to Earp, Holliday might be the second most recognizable name among the legends of the West, and yet several details of his life remain sketchy. *The Icons of the Wild West* chronicles Holliday's life, while also analyzing his legacy and the mythology that has enveloped his story. Along with pictures of important people, places, and events in his life, you will learn about Doc Holliday like you never have before, in no time at all.

Jesse James (1847-1882)

"There is a hell of excitement in this part of the country." – Jesse James

The Wild West has made legends out of many men after their deaths, but like Wild Bill Hickok, Jesse James was a celebrity during his life. However, while Hickok was (mostly) a lawman, Jesse James was and remains the most famous outlaw of the Wild West, with both his life of crime and his death remaining pop culture fixtures.

James and his notorious older brother Frank were Confederate bushwhackers in the lawless region of Missouri during the Civil War. Despite being a teenager, James was severely wounded twice during the war, including being shot in the chest, but that would hardly slow him down after the war ended. As he recuperated, some of the men he was known to associate with during the war robbed Clay County Savings Bank in Liberty, Missouri in 1866. While it's still unclear whether James was involved, he was soon conducting his own bank robberies.

Young Jesse became notorious in 1869 after robbing the Daviess County Savings Association in Gallatin, Missouri, during which he murdered the bank cashier in the mistaken belief that the cashier was Union officer Samuel Cox. Despite being officially branded an outlaw, public resentment with government corruption and the banks helped turn James into a celebrated "Robin Hood" type of robber, despite the fact he never actually gave anyone money.

Eventually James, his brother and their infamous gang became the most hunted outlaws in the country, but Jesse would famously be done in by the brother of his most trusted gang members. After Jesse moved in with the Ford brothers, Bob Ford began secretly negotiating turning in the famous outlaw to Missouri Governor Thomas Crittenden. On April 3, 1882, as the gang prepared for another robber, Jesse was famously shot in the back of the head by Bob Ford as he stood on a chair fixing a painting. While conspiracy theories have continued to linger that somehow James was not killed on that day, the Ford brothers would celebrate their participation in his murder, Bob himself would be murdered a few years later, and Jesse James's legacy had been ensured.

The Icons of the Wild West chronicles the outlaw's life, while also analyzing his legacy and the mythology that has enveloped his story, attempting to separate fact from fiction to determine what the notorious robber was really like. Along with pictures of important people, places, and events in his life, you will learn about Jesse James like you never have before, in no time at all.

Billy the Kid (1859-1881)

"I'm not afraid to die like a man fighting, but I would not like to be killed like a dog unarmed." – Billy the Kid

In many ways, the narrative of the Wild West has endured more as legend than reality, and a perfect example of that can be found in the legend of William Henry McCarty Jr., better known as William H. Bonney or "Billy the Kid". Indeed, separating fact from fiction when it comes to the life of the West's most famous outlaw is nearly impossible, due in great measure to the fact that the young man himself cultivated the image of a deadly outlaw and legendary gunman himself. Though Billy the Kid may have killed anywhere from 4-9 men in his short life, he was often credited for killing more than 20.

With a wit as quick as his trigger, Billy the Kid had a bullet and a wisecrack for every man he killed, and his notoriety only grew when exaggerated accounts of his actions in Lincoln County eventually earned The Kid a bounty on his head. In December 1880, an ambitious buffalo hunter (and future Sheriff), Pat Garrett, helped track down and capture the famous outlaw, only for Billy the Kid to somehow escape jail shortly before his scheduled execution.

There was plenty of gunplay in the outlaw's life to help him become a well known if not celebrated figure in the West, but the legendary and controversial nature of his death has also helped him endure. A few months after his escape from jail, Billy the Kid was hunted down by Garrett in New Mexico once again, and it's still not completely clear whether The Kid was killed by Garrett in self-defense or simply murdered outright.

The Icons of the Wild West chronicles The Kid's life, while also analyzing his legacy and the mythology that has enveloped his story, attempting to separate fact from fiction to determine what the frontier legend was really like. Along with pictures of important people, places, and events in his life, you will learn about Billy the Kid like you never have before, in no time at all.

Butch Cassidy (1866-1908)

The Wild West has made legends out of many men through the embellishment of their stories, such as crediting Billy the Kid and Wild Bill Hickok for killing far more people than they actually did. But it has also made icons out of outlaws like Butch Cassidy and the Sundance Kid based on the mystery and uncertainty surrounding their crimes and deaths, allowing speculation and legend to fill in the gaps.

Alongside Jesse James, Robert LeRoy Parker has become remembered as Butch Cassidy, one of the most notorious outlaws of the west. Though he is commonly associated with the Sundance Kid, the duo had a full-fledged gang known as the Wild Bunch conducting robberies in the Southwest, and they became legendary for their shootouts and their escapes from the law. Eventually, Butch Cassidy and his most famous acquaintance fled as far east as New York City and as far south as Argentina.

In fact, it was in South America that Butch Cassidy and the Sundance Kid are believed to have met their ultimate fate, in yet another shootout with Bolivian soldiers. The mystery and controversy surrounding that shootout (and whether the two bandits were actually them) have helped ensure their place in Western lore, and as with so many other legends of the West, people continue to speculate that Butch Cassidy and the Sundance Kid survived and lived out the rest of their lives.

The Icons of the Wild West chronicles the outlaw's life, while also analyzing his legacy and the mythology that has enveloped his story, attempting to separate fact from fiction to determine what the notorious robber was really like. Along with pictures of important people, places, and events in his life, you will learn about Butch Cassidy like you never have before, in no time at all.

Wild Bill Hickok

Chapter 1: Hickok's Early Years

Childhood

James Butler Hickok was born on May 2, 1837 in Homer, Illinois to parents that had a clear sense of right and wrong. The English farm family, which could trace its heritage back to William Shakespeare, was part of the growing anti-slavery faction that was emerging in the decades before the Civil War. By the time Oliver and Polly Hickok's son James was born, the underground railroad had been providing safe havens in the North for slaves fleeing the South for over a decade. The Hickok farmhouse, where Oliver and Polly raised six children, eventually became one of the stops on the underground railroad into north-central Illinois, about 90 miles southwest of Chicago.

This memorial marks the site of Wild Bill's childhood home

Oliver Hickok owned his own store until the financial crisis of 1837, which forced him to do neighborhood chores just to make a living. James worked in the neighborhood, too, when he was old enough to do so, although he found that he preferred shooting game to feed the family instead of plowing farmland. He was good at it, too. Young James showed such a propensity for handling guns that it was not long before he was an expert marksman, a talent his community couldn't help but notice either. A voracious reader, James soaked up the stories of the legends of the frontier, such as Kit Carson and Daniel Boone, and like many young men who grew up on the Plains, the expansive West held great allure. It represented freedom, open land, and opportunity.

Independent in spirit, James left his Illinois home after his father died on May 5, 1852, when he was still just a teenager. Family members report that his mother Polly was as independent and strong-willed as he was, and their clash led to James wasting little time in setting out away from home. But the young teen's desire to get out of town may also have been partially motivated by a brawl that he had with another young man named Charlie Hudson in 1855. James and Charlie were mule drivers for the canal boats on the Illinois and Michigan Canal in LaSalle, Illinois. James reportedly got into a fight with Charlie and both boys fell into the canal. When James saw only bubbles and no body float to the surface of the water, he mistakenly assumed that Charlie had drowned and fled the scene. It was not long after that that he and his brother, Lorenzo, went to St. Louis, but when they got there, a letter was waiting for them, telling them that Polly was sick. James thought it was a ploy by Hudson's family or the authorities to get him to go back home and wouldn't go, but Lorenzo returned to Illinois. Instead, James took a steamboat to Leavenworth, Kansas.

Polly Hickok lived to be 74 years old. She died in Troy Grove – formerly known as Homer – in 1878, two years after her son's murder.

Bleeding Kansas

Throughout the 1850s, American politicians tried to sort out the nation's intractable issues. In an attempt to organize the center of North America – Kansas and Nebraska – without offsetting the slave-free balance, Senator Stephen Douglas of Illinois proposed the Kansas-Nebraska Act. The Kansas-Nebraska Act eliminated the Missouri Compromise line of 1820, which the Compromise of 1850 had maintained. The Missouri Compromise had stipulated that states north of the boundary line determined in that bill would be free, and that states south of it *could* have slavery. This was essential to maintaining the balance of slave and free states in the Union. The Kansas-Nebraska Act, however, ignored the line completely and proposed that all new territories be organized by popular sovereignty. Settlers could vote whether they wanted their state to be slave or free.

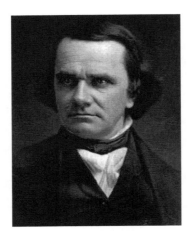

Stephen Douglas, "The Little Giant"

When popular sovereignty became the standard in Kansas and Nebraska, the primary result was that thousands of zealous pro-slavery and anti-slavery advocates both moved to Kansas to influence the vote, creating a dangerous (and ultimately deadly) mix. Numerous attacks took place between the two sides. Neighboring Missouri, a slave state, tried to intimidate Kansans into taking a pro-slavery position and battled against the Free-Staters who wanted Kansas to enter the Union as free state. Many pro-slavery Missourians organized attacks on Kansas towns just across the border. Horace Greeley, editor of the *New York Tribune*, labeled the conflict between the Free-Staters and the Border Ruffians from Missouri as "Bleeding Kansas."

The best known abolitionist in Bleeding Kansas was a middle aged man named John Brown. A radical abolitionist, Brown organized a small band of like-minded followers and fought with the armed groups of pro-slavery men in Kansas for several months, including a notorious incident known as the Pottawatomie Massacre, in which Brown's supporters murdered five men. Over 50 people died before John Brown left the territory, which ultimately entered the Union as a free state in 1859.

John Brown

In 1855, Hickok served as bodyguard to General James Lane of Indiana, who led a group of abolitionists and was considered by many to be the leader of the Jayhawks, a militant Free-Stater group. Lane became one of Kansas's first senators when it was admitted to the Union as a free state in 1861. It was also during this time that Hickok met Isaac and Mary Cody, both Free-Staters. Isaac, who had been injured in a fight with a Border Ruffian, died from pneumonia and kidney disease in April 1857. Hickok befriended 10 year-old Bill Cody, known in Western lore as Buffalo Bill Cody, and the two became life-long friends.

By early 1857, Hickok had moved to the village of Monticello, about 25 miles from Leavenworth, Kansas, where he became friends with John Owen, who had married a Shawnee Indian named Patinuxa. The 20 year-old Hickok had a brief romance with their teenage daughter, Mary, but when Hickok's mother found out that her son was involved with an Indian, she sent Lorenzo to Kansas to put an end to the relationship. Hickok reluctantly complied with his mother's wishes, but he stayed in Monticello, where he was elected town constable in March 1858. It was here that he also started being referred to as William, or Bill, although the reasons are not clear. What is clear is that the violence and lawlessness he witnessed bothered him. In letters home, he wrote about what he saw and was convinced that Kansas was not safe for women and children until law enforcement was in place.

Those sentiments would prove ironic considering Hickok would spend much of his life on both sides of the violence and lawlessness that troubled him so much as a young adult.

Chapter 2: Nebraska and the Murder of Dave McCanles

Russell, Majors, and Waddell was a transportation company based in Lexington, Missouri that was created to supply military posts in the West and Southwest. In addition to operating stagecoaches, the company is credited with starting the Pony Express mail service. When the Mexican War ended in 1848, the United States Army needed a method for transporting goods from the new depot in Santa Fe, New Mexico to six new posts in New Mexico Territory.

When the government awarded its initial contracts, Russell, Majors and Waddell was one of the first companies to get one, and at first it paid off. However, in 1857, the quartermaster at Leavenworth asked the company to move far more freight than it was contracted for to Salt Lake City. The company, afraid of jeopardizing its contract, borrowed money to fulfill the request. While waiting for reimbursement from the government, a series of other devastating financial decisions put the company in dire financial straits.

In April 1861, Russell, Majors, and Waddell bought a ranch owned by Dave McCanles in Rock Creek, Nebraska, which they then rented out and used as a Pony Express relay station for their Overland Stage Company. The agreement was one-third down and the remainder of the balance spread out over the next three months. By this time, the company's financial problems were no secret, especially to its drivers and other employees.

For reasons that are under dispute, Hickok was also in Rock Creek about this same time, and legend has it that while working as a stage driver for Russell, Majors, and Waddell, Hickok fought off a grizzly bear in the Raton Pass in New Mexico and was sent to Rock Creek to recuperate. According to Hickok himself, when his path was blocked by a bear and its two cubs, he confronted the bear and shot it in the head, but the bullet only ricocheted off the skull and further angered it. Hickok then colorfully claimed that the bear began crushing him, while he managed to shoot one paw and then slash the bear's throat with his knife. Hickok's incredible account is disputed by Hickok biographer Joseph Rosa, who has asserted that not only was there no fight with a grizzly bear but that Hickok was actually working for the stage company Jones and Cartwright.

Whatever the reasons for Hickok being in Rock Creek, he and McCanles were quickly at odds. McCanles was known as a local bully, always looking for a way to make a buck. It has also been claimed that McCanles was part of the McCanles Gang or McCandless Gang, a gang of outlaws wanted for various crimes including robbery, horse theft, and even murder.

McCanles owned a toll bridge that he had sold many times over, reclaiming it from the buyers who did not meet his strict stipulations. He also took what appeared to be an immediate dislike to Hickok. Part of Hickok's legend was his appearance. He was noted for his piercing gray eyes and long, flowing blonde hair, which was a typical hairstyle for plainsmen of that time. He dressed well, often with his guns stowed in a sash rather than holsters, and was tall, trim, and athletic. Some of the more famous photos of him show him dressed in buckskin. McCanles also derisively mocked Hickok as "Duck Bill," an insulting reference to Hickok's nose and outward protruding upper lip, and it's been suggested that Hickok grew his famous mustache afterward to hide it. Tensions between the two men were not eased when Hickok began to see Kate Shell, a woman that also interested McCanles despite the fact that he was already married.

Not surprisingly, given the company's financial troubles, Overland Stage fell behind in its payments to McCanles. On the afternoon of July 12, 1860, McCanles went with his son and two employees to the ranch to tell the superintendent, Horace Wellman, that he wanted the ranch returned to him for nonpayment. Wellman refused and retreated back into the ranch house as his daughter Jane argued with McCanles over the way he spoke to her father. Hickok appeared, briefly taking up Jane's cause before getting McCanles water, as he requested. Hickok then went back into the ranch house behind a curtained area, where Wellman was getting a gun. McCanles called to Hickok to come back and shortly after that, McCanles was shot and killed. It is not clear whether the shot came from Hickok or Wellman. Both of McCanles's employees were also shot, and one was killed when Wellman's wife attacked him with a hoe. The second employee was found bleeding in the bushes and was shot again, this time fatally.

McCanles's son, Monroe, who rushed to his father's side as he died, claims that Hickok killed McCanles. Wellman's wife would have tried to kill Monroe, too, had he not run away. Questions that remain unanswered are whether or not McCanles and his men were armed and who actually fired the fatal shots. Hickok, Wellman, and another Pony Express rider who joined the fray, Doc Brink, were all arrested. In their trial in Beatrice, Nebraska, they claimed that the shootings were done in the defense of company property and a judge dismissed the murder charges.

The McCanles incident has become one of the best known stories of Wild Bill's life, and there is no shortage of varying accounts. Some accounts have claimed Hickok shot McCanles and both of his employees, while Monroe later claimed it was Wellman who shot his father, "Probably the motive for killing was fear. Father had told Mrs. Wellman to tell her husband to come out. The Wellmans were the folks who lived there and kept the station. She said he wouldn't and father said if he wouldn't come out he would go in and drag him out. I think rather than be man-handled, he killed father."

One relay station foreman told an interesting anecdote about Hickok's journey to his trial. "At the time of this affair I was at a station farther west and reached this station just as Wild Bill was getting ready to go to Beatrice for his trial. He wanted me to go with him and as we started on our way, imagine my surprise and uncomfortable feeling when he announced his intention of stopping at the McCanles home. I would have rather been somewhere else, but Bill stopped. He told Mrs. McCanles he was sorry he had to kill her man then took out $35.00 (2010:US$839) and gave it to her saying: 'This is all I have, sorry I do not have more to give you.' We drove on to Beatrice and at the trial, his plea was self-defense, no one appeared against him and he was cleared. The trial did not last more than fifteen minutes".

In 1883, D.M. Kelsey published *Our Pioneer Heroes and Their Daring Deeds*, which not only contained a brief biography of Hickok but also claimed to have Hickok's own accounts of certain events in his life. In that book, Wild Bill is credited with killing six of the ten members of the McCanles Gang, and he is quoted as saying, "I remember that one of them struck me with his gun, and I got hold of a knife, and then I got kind o' wild like, and it was all cloudy, and I struck savage blows, following the devils up from one side of the room to the other and into the corners, striking and slashing until I knew every one was dead."

Regardless of what actually happened, and the true extent of Hickok's involvement, a cornerstone of his legend was now in place. With that, he headed back to Leavenworth, as word spread quickly that Hickok was not a man to be reckoned with.

Chapter 3: Civil War and the Hickok-Tutt Shootout

Always a Union man, Hickok signed on as a wagonmaster with the Union army in Sedalia, Missouri in October 1861, but records indicate he left that position within a year. It's unclear where Hickok was for the next year, but he later spent time as a guide and scout for General Samuel P. Curtis. Speculation is that he got his nickname "Wild Bill" because of his daring escapes from enemy territory during his time as a spy, venturing alone into Confederate territory. Others say that when he was saving a bartender from a lynching in Kansas City in 1861, a woman in the crowd shouted, "Good for you, Wild Bill." However, there were so many stories told about him after the war and after he became a household name that it is hard to know what was fact and what was fiction.

In late 1863 Hickok became provost marshal of southwest Missouri as a member of the Springfield, MO detective police. Hickok kept himself busy with menial tasks like hassling Union soldiers found drinking on duty, checking liquor licenses, and tracking down debtors. By 1864, Hickok seemed to have resigned and was hired by General John B. Sanborn that year as a scout, receiving five dollars a day plus a horse and equipment. It's also believed that due to his abilities as a marksman, he served as a sharpshooter at the Battle of Pea Ridge in Arkansas in 1864.

The Hickok-Tutt Shootout

As the war drew to an end in 1865, the first men to be relieved of duty were scouts and spies, leaving Hickok without work. He settled in Springfield, Missouri, where he became a regular at the gambling tables. He was also rarely without a drink. In 1883, a History of Greene County, Missouri was published, and it described Hickok in Springfield as "by nature a ruffian... a drunken, swaggering fellow, who delighted when 'on a spree' to frighten nervous men and timid women."

A frequent gambling companion was Davis Tutt, who also served in the Civil War as a Confederate. Records indicate, though, that Tutt may have deserted the Confederacy for the Union, which could explain how he ended up in Springfield as a friend of Hickok.

During a poker game in July 1865, Tutt pressed Hickok for money he owed for a prior debt. Some suggest that the cause of the new tension between the two former friends was a woman named Susanna Moore. Hickok had a relationship with her, but during a falling-out, Tutt stepped in to console her. Hickok then supposedly struck up a relationship with Tutt's sister, which upset not only Tutt but also Tutt's mother, who was still a Confederate woman with hard feelings about Union men. Some accounts even claim Hickok had impregnated her.

Whatever the reason for the falling out, Tutt was now unabashedly helping Hickok's opponents at the table in an attempt to bankrupt him. However, Hickok was doing well at the table that night and paid Tutt the $40 Tutt claimed he owed. Tutt then said that Hickok owed him another $35 for a gambling debt. Hickok replied – politely, by all accounts – that he thought it was only $25 and that he would check his notes. Tutt saw Hickok's watch on the table and took it, saying he was keeping it as collateral until he got his $35. Hickok was enraged, but he was also outmanned and outgunned by Tutt and his friends around the table, so he warned Tutt that he had better not see him wearing the watch.

Over the next several days, Tutt's friends constantly attempted to goad Hickok into a confrontation, When a group of Tutt's friends told Hickok that Tutt was going to wear the watch in the middle of the town square the next day, Hickok reportedly replied, "He shouldn't come across that square unless dead men can walk." That night, Hickok returned to his room and prepared his guns.

On the morning of July 21, Tutt walked around the town square openly displaying Hickok's watch. According to witnesses, Hickok confronted Tutt in the square and attempted to negotiate the return of the watch for the debt of $25, but Tutt demanded $45, upping the price. When no deal was reached, it was said the two both went for a drink, but Tutt soon came back to the square still wearing Hickok's watch.

Around 6:00 p.m. that night, one of the few true quick draw duels in the history of the West took place. As Hickok strode into the public square, he yelled at Tutt, "Dave, here I am", cocked his pistol, and warned him, "Don't you come across here with that watch." Tutt did not respond, instead putting his hand on his pistol. A showdown was now inevitable. Concerned townspeople ducked behind corners and buildings as the duel was about to start.

Though these kinds of duels would be portrayed countless times in the movies as two shooters standing face to face, the duel actually started with the two men standing side by side at a distance of about 75 yards. After both men briefly hesitated, they both drew their revolvers at the same time. Hickok rested his revolver along his arm, and eyewitnesses claimed they both shot around the same time, but Tutt's shot went over Hickok's head while Hickok's shot hit Tutt square in the chest. After gasping out to his friends "Boys, I'm killed", and staggering into the nearby courthouse, Tutt died.

Hickok was arrested and charged with murder and later manslaughter under the name William Haycocke, the name he'd been using in Springfield. His trial began on August 3 and lasted three days, during which nearly two dozen witnesses told different accounts on whether both men fired, who fired first, and whether Tutt fired at all. Hickok claimed self-defense, which should not have been possible since he came to the square expecting to duel, but the jury still found his shooting of Tutt justified. As one historian noted, "Nothing better described the times than the fact that dangling a watch held as security for a poker debt was widely regarded as a justifiable provocation for resorting to firearms."

Harper's New Monthly Creates a Legend

Hickok was a locally known personality in the Kansas/Missouri region by the end of 1865, notorious for being a fearless gunman and a deadly accurate shooter. However, after George Ward Nichols arrived in Springfield in September to write an article on Wild Bill for a *Harper's New Monthly* story, Hickok was a folk hero on his way to becoming a household name. Nichols was an Army man from Cincinnati, Ohio, and Captain Richard Bentley Owen introduced Nichols to Hickok. Owen was well acquainted with Hickok, who worked for Owen as a scout and spy during the Civil War and after the war in Fort Riley, Kansas. Owen also paid Hickok's $2,000 bail during the Tutt trial. Nichols interviewed both Owen and Hickok for a feature story for *Harper's New Monthly Magazine.*

When the article ran as the lead in the magazine's February 1867 issue, complete with portraits of Wild Bill with his flowing locks, it caused a stir across the nation. The magazine's East Coast readers could not get enough of the tales of the wild gunman of the West, helped along by *The New York Tribune* making a sensation with excerpts from the article. In Kansas, many were pleased to have one of their own talked about in print and the magazine was a hot seller, but in Springfield, the locals were less pleased with the characterization of their citizens as dirty, backwards, and ill-mannered. The editor of Springfield's newspaper, *The Patriot*, wrote in the January 31 issue that many would recall Nichols, who "was here for a few days in the summer of 1865, splurging around our 'strange, half-civilized people,' seriously endangering the supply of

---

[1] Joseph G. Rosa. "George Ward Nichols and the Legend of Wild Bill Hickok." *Arizona and the West.*

lager and corn whiskey, and putting on more airs than a spotted stud horse in the ring of a county fair." The editor went on to say that if Nichols were to return to town, a good share of the people "will kick him wherever met, for lying like a dog upon the city and people of Springfield."[1]

The article was not completely inaccurate, although it did refer to Hickok as "William," rather than James. The tales about the McCanles and Tutt shootings occurred mostly as described. It was also probably true that Hickok was such a good shot with his Colt that he could fire six balls into a target 50 yards away. Modern shooters attest that the Colt was notable for its accuracy at long-range and that this feat is a good show of marksmanship, although not superior. The liberties that the article took in describing Hickok's horse, Black Nell – she supposedly would do tricks on Hickok's command – and even with Hickok's grammar, which was dumbed down to a clownish stereotype of a hillbilly, fueled criticism about the article for years to come. However, it is possible that it was not Nichols who exaggerated the tales of Hickok, but rather it could have been the magazine editors, trying to fluff up the piece to stir interest.

The article also included clearly outlandish information about "Wild Bill Hitchcock", claiming he had killed hundreds of men. The stories were so exaggerated that some Western papers felt compelled to publish rebuttals.

The legends and myth of Hickok grew later that year when Hickok was interviewed in St. Louis by H.M. Stanley, the same Stanley who famously located the medical missionary Dr. Livingstone in Africa. The article that appeared in the *St. Louis Democrat* in March 1867 gave Hickok's quote about the number of men he had hilled at well over a hundred. At this point, Hickok had killed Tutt and possibly some of the McCanles gang.

Nevertheless, dime novels featuring Wild Bill followed soon after that. "Wild Bill the Indian Slayer" was published in July 1867 and "Wild Bill's First Trail" came out in February 1868. He was also featured as Buffalo Bill's trusty companion in stories about Bill Cody. Hickok did his part to live up to his own image as a Western icon. His buckskin outfits were straight out of a story about Daniel Boone, not something one would typically see on the Plains, but he made sure to be seen on train platforms dressed that way when people from the East disembarked.

Harper's illustration in an 1867 issue depicts Wild Bill threatening Tutt's friend after shooting Tutt.

Chapter 4: Wild Bill's Career in Law Enforcement

Hays City, Kansas

Wild Bill tried to embellish his legend in 1867 by exaggerating an encounter with Indians. Eyewitnesses documented an incident in May of that year in which Hickok was scouting near Fort Harker, Kansas when he was confronted by a large group of Indians and apparently shot a few of them. That July, Hickok gave an account to a reporter that he had led a group of men in pursuit of Indians and killed 10 of them and took 5 prisoner. While contemporaries confirmed the group rode out to find the Indians, they claimed Wild Bill's group returned "without nary a dead Indian, [never] even seeing a live one".

Wild Bill may have become a legend of the West in 1867, but he seemed ready to give it up that same year by moving to Niagara Falls. About as far removed as possible from the frontier, Hickok tried acting in a stage play called "The Daring Buffalo Chasers of the Plains", but he was so awful as an actor that he quickly made his way back west.

Between 1867 and 1870, Hickok worked periodically as a deputy marshal in Hays City, Kansas, and on August 23, 1869, Hickok won a special election for Ellis County sheriff. The people of Hays City had grown tired of the lawlessness of the buffalo soldiers and teamsters that congregated in the town, and with his reputation preceding him, it was hoped that Hickok's presence would restore some law and order. He made an imposing baseball umpire, too. He had learned to play during the Civil War and was a big fan of the game, which was as wild as the West in the late 1800s. Hickok was especially a fan of the Kansas City Antelopes, and during one game in 1868, he reportedly umpired with both of his Colts strapped to his hip, just in case there were any disputed calls.

Hickok took his new appointment as marshal seriously and was well armed for battle. He wore his two Colt revolvers butt forward as always, allowing him to quick draw in the reverse "twist" style used by cavalrymen. He also carried a Bowie knife and was often seen carrying a sawed off shotgun. Hickok had a strong presence, even without the guns, but as sheriff, he could frighten some people just by looking at them with his steely stare.

Perhaps not surprisingly, it was not long into his tenure before trouble found Wild Bill, who shot and killed two men within the first month of being sheriff. One eyewitness described the first shooting of Bill Mulvey: "I was standing near Wild Bill on Main Street, when someone 'began shooting up the town' at the eastern end of the street. It was Bill Mulvey, a notorious murderer from Missouri, known as a handy man with a gun... Mulvey appeared on the scene, tearing toward us on his iron grey horse, rifle in hand, full cocked. When Wild Bill saw Mulvey, he walked out to meet him, apparently waving his hand to some fellows behind Mulvey and calling to them: 'Don't shoot him in the back; he is drunk'. Mulvey stopped his horse and, wheeling the animal about, drew a bead on his rifle in the direction of the imaginary man he thought Wild Bill was addressing. But before he realized the ruse that had been played upon him, Wild Bill had aimed his six-shooter and fired – just once. Mulvey dropped from his horse – dead, the bullet having penetrated his temple and then passed through his head."

Then, in September 1869, Hickok and his deputy heard that a local ruffian named Samuel Strawhun and a gang of his drunken pals were causing a commotion at John Bitter's Beer Saloon. When Hickok arrived at the saloon, he paused to gather a bunch of glasses that the desperadoes had left outside of the bar. When he deposited them back on the bar, Strawhun said that if anyone tried to interfere with his fun, he would shoot them. With that, he grabbed one of the glasses from the bar, held it up as if to throw it, and Hickok shot him, killing him instantly. The chaos was quelled, but some eyebrows were raised at Hickok's method. The town had hired him to maintain law and order, but now they wondered if they got more than they bargained for from a man who was supposed to help keep the peace. Nevertheless, a jury found the shooting justifiable.

Cowboys and outlaws weren't the only ones who found themselves on the wrong end of Hickok's guns. In July 1870, Hickok found himself in a gunfight with some disorderly soldiers of the 7th U.S. Cavalry, the regiment that would become infamous later in that decade at Little Bighorn. Two of the cavalrymen, Jeremiah Lonergan and John Kyle, confronted Hickok in a saloon in Hays, with Lonergan pinning Hickock down on the ground while Kyle aimed the gun at Hickock's head and fired. Luckily for Wild Bill, the gun misfired, at which point Hickok reached for his own guns, shooting Lonergan in the knee and mortally wounding Kyle with two shots.

Given the manner in which trouble constantly found the man charged with keeping the peace, it's no surprise that Hickok failed to be reelected when his first term in law enforcement was over.

Abilene, Kansas

In 1871, Abilene, Kansas was having its own crime problem. Cattle baron Joe McCoy had virtually built the town from the ground up, constructing a hotel, a bank, a stockyard, and an office building. Through much advertising on his part, McCoy was successful in getting Texas ranchers to drive their cattle through Abilene, but where there was money, there were also con artists, thieves, prostitutes, and rowdy cowboys. McCoy hired an experienced lawman to help with the crime, but his marshal, Thomas "Bear River" Smith, was killed in the line of duty and the deputy had done little to win the confidence of Abilene citizens.

Smith had been mortally wounded in a shootout trying to arrest Andrew McConnell and Moses Miles, the latter of which decapitated him with an axe.

On April 15, 1871, the Abilene town council approved the hiring of Hickok as their new marshal. Hickok earned $150 per month plus 25 percent of fines collected and an extra 50 cents for every stray dog he killed. Again, Hickok was hired for his reputation more than his skills as a lawman. He was lax in his enforcement of the no-guns rule in town, but nobody wanted to challenge him on it. What really concerned the townspeople was that their sheriff spent more than his fair share of time at the poker table, though. With a steady job, Susanna Moore reunited with Hickok, but she later left when he was giving more attention to the women in the local brothels.

Despite these issues, Hickok was tough on the cowboys, which is what McCoy wanted. In one incident, when asked to retrieve a local man who was avoiding a court appearance, Hickok picked him up like a sack of potatoes and carried him over his shoulder to the courthouse.

Naturally, the well known law man had made enemies in town, including outlaw John Wesley Hardin, a notorious gunfighter who is known to have killed at least 27 men during his life. Hardin claimed that after the marshal tried to arrest him for having pistols in town, he used a "road agent spin" to disarm Hickok, a story almost certainly exaggerated if not outright fabricated. Hardin also claimed Hickok begrudgingly admired him and later befriended him, but in August 1871 Hardin left town after Hickok came looking for him in connection with the murder of a man in a hotel in Abilene that had committed the cardinal offense of snoring too loud during the night.

Hardin

Another man Hickok had issues with was Phil Coe, a Texas gambler and owner of the Bull's Head Tavern who had developed bad blood with the new marshal. The Bull's Head Tavern had painted a picture of a fully erect bull as an advertisement, causing some to complain about it to Hickok. When Hickok's request to remove the advertisement was rejected, Hickok took to altering it himself, infuriating Coe and Ben Thompson, the two men running the tavern. Before Hardin left town, Hardin claimed Thompson had tried to incite him into confronting Hickok, telling him, "He's a damn Yankee. Picks on Rebels, especially Texans, to kill." Hardin reportedly responded, "If Wild Bill needs killin', why don't you kill him yourself?" It's also been claimed that Coe threatened Hickok himself by claiming he could "kill a crow on the wing", to which Hickok reportedly (though probably apocryphally) responded, "Did the crow have a pistol? Was he shooting back? I will be."

On the night of October 5, 1871, during the middle of a brawl being watched by a crowd of people, including Hickok, Phil Coe fired a shot outside of the Alamo Saloon. Hickok felt like enforcing the law about having guns within city limits this night, no doubt based on who fired the shot, and when Hickok ordered him arrested, Coe claimed he was firing at a stray dog before quickly wheeling and aiming his gun at Hickok. Some claimed Coe fired two shots and missed, while others claim Hickok fired first.

Meanwhile, Hickok's occasional deputy, a Kansas City bartender named Mike Williams, was expected to return to Kansas City later that evening, but when he heard the chaos outside of the Alamo, he headed to Hickok's aid. Hickok caught a glimpse of someone rushing forward, and since he did not realize it was Williams, Hickok turned and fired two shots instinctively, killing his own deputy and friend. A distraught Hickok paid for funeral expenses and went to Kansas City to explain what had happened to Williams' widow, but Hickok regretted the incident for the rest of his life. Coe died of his wounds three days later.

It was Hickok's last stint in law enforcement and his last gunfight. Abilene's town council announced that there would be no more cattle drives through its town, and with that there would be no more need for a strong-arm sheriff. Hickok was relieved of his duties two months after the Coe shooting and embarked on an entirely different career.

As an example of the way in which events of Wild Bill's life were twisted and embellished after his death, Abilene mayor Theophilus Little wrote of his time in Abilene in a notebook hat eventually made its way to the Abilene Historical Society. In 1911, Little wrote glowingly of Hickok and recounted the Coe shooting: "Phil Coe was from Texas, ran the 'Bull's Head', a saloon and gambling den, sold whiskey and men's souls. As vile a character as I ever met, for some cause Wild Bill incurred Coe's hatred and he vowed to secure the death of the marshall. Not having the courage to do it himself, he one day filled about 200 cowboys with whiskey intending to get them into trouble with Wild Bill, hoping that they would get to shooting and in the melee shoot the marshal. But Coe "reckoned without his host". Wild Bill had learned of the scheme and cornered Coe, had his two pistols drawn on Coe. Just as he pulled the trigger one of the policemen rushed around the corner between Coe and the pistols and both balls entered his body, killing him instantly. In an instant, he pulled the triggers again, sending two bullets into Coe's abdomen (Coe lived a day or two) and whirling with his two guns drawn on the drunken crowd of cowboys, "and now do any of you fellows want the rest of these bullets." Not a word was uttered."

Chapter 5: Wild Bill in Show Business

With law enforcement behind him, Hickok turned to his favorite pastimes – women, drinking, and gambling. However, the nation was still fascinated with Hickok and the West. Sensing an opportunity to cash in, he took Colonel Sidney Barnett up on his offer to stage a buffalo chase in Niagara Falls, New York. Hickok and his associates rounded up six buffalo from Nebraska and loaded them on to an eastbound train. The idea was to charge admission to watch Hickok hunt the buffalo, but there were several problems, not the least of which was only a fraction of the crowd they expected showed up and they forgot to charge admission. Hickok ended up passing a hat for donations, but he lost money in the end.

One person in the crowd was his old friend, Bill Cody. He saw the crowd respond to the cowboys lassoing the longhorns and the Indian war dances. He also saw how people responded to Wild Bill. Cody began to dress like Wild Bill and would draw from the show in Niagara Falls to create his own Wild West show, which became a famous sensation for several years. At this point, Cody was not as famous as Wild Bill, but he was making a name for himself back East as an actor. He had been performing in a touring western show, "Scouts of the Prairie," based on a play written by Ned Buntline. Buntline had wanted to write about Hickok, but Hickok chased him off with his Colt when Buntline approached him at a saloon, so Buntline wrote about Cody instead, keeping Hickok as a supporting character.

By all accounts, the acting in the stage show was terrible, but audiences loved it anyway, eager to take part in just about anything related to the mythical West. After Hickok's disaster in Niagara Falls, he was broke. In Kansas City, he was arrested as a vagrant when he caused a disturbance after demanding that a band at a concert in the park stop playing "Dixie." Destitute, he took his old friend up on his offer when Cody suggested that he go east and play the part of himself in the new show, "Scouts of the Plains." He joined the troupe on July 27, 1873 with its stars Buffalo Bill Cody and John B. "Texas Jack" Omohundro. The show was as equally bad as "Scouts of the Prairie," but it was just as big of a hit in the cities and towns of New York and Pennsylvania.

Wild Bill, Texas Jack Omohundro, and Buffalo Bill Cody in 1873

To say that Hickok was a bad actor is an understatement. His strong, clear speaking voice came out weak and timid on stage. He often forgot his lines, a condition not helped by the fact that he took several sips of whiskey to help his courage before going on stage. When he forgot his lines, he often resorted to stepping out of character and telling jokes with the crowd. Not surprisingly, Hickok hated acting and thought that he and his fellow actors were making fools of themselves. He complained about the stage lights and what he thought they might do to his vision, and he did not like the schmoozing that went along with a show business career. Cody wrote in his memoirs that Hickok only stuck with it because of the money, although Hickok made no secret of the fact that he did not appreciate getting paid less than Cody and Texas Jack.

Hickok amused himself on tour by firing blanks at the "supers" who played the parts of the Indians in the show. This not only caused some serious burns on the men, but it often brought the show to a quick and abrupt halt. Despite being asked to stop shooting at the other actors, he refused. Cody told him he would have to leave the production if it continued. Hickok responded by simply going backstage, gathering his things, and leaving word with the stagehand that he would not be back. When asked by a reporter why he left, Hickok said that he had an urgent telegram from General Phil Sheridan, asking him to be a scout for his troupe at Fort Laramie. This was a lie, devised by Hickok to save face. After five months, with his acting career behind him, he headed west again.

Chapter 6: Deadwood and Hickok's Final Days

Agnes Lake

In 1847, Agnes Mersman married Bill Lake Thatcher, a well-known circus performer whose stage name was simply Bill Lake. Young Agnes was a talented performer in her own right and shortly after marrying Bill, she made her circus debut on the floating wire, a precursor to the famed high wire of circus acts. Also a skilled lion tamer, she was such a talent that it did not take long for her to take the top billing in their act. When Agnes returned from a tour of Europe, she and Bill bought their own circus and took it on the road. It was a family affair, featuring several children that the couple adopted. It all came to an end, though, in Granby, Missouri in 1869 when a man tried to sneak in to catch a performance without paying. When Bill confronted him, the man shot and killed him.

Agnes carried on with the circus despite her tragic loss. In 1871, her circus passed through Abilene, Kansas, where she made the acquaintance of the town marshal, Wild Bill Hickok. Agnes's life took her on the road, though, so there was little chance that she could stay in Abilene and see what might develop with Hickok, but they wrote to each other often. Their paths crossed again in 1873 when her circus went to Rochester, New York. By coincidence, Hickok was there, too, in his brief tenure as an actor.

The pair continued to write but did not see each other again until 1876 in Cheyenne, Wyoming. Agnes had just left San Francisco and had stopped in Cheyenne to visit friends. She was now a wealthy woman, having sold the circus, and was awaiting the birth of her first grandchild from her daughter, Emma. Hickok had drifted in and out of Cheyenne since leaving the East Coast, filling his time with gambling, hunting, and trapping. The man that Agnes saw in Cheyenne is not the man she first met in Abilene. No longer was Hickok a feared gunman, but rather he told stories in saloons about the good old days for the price of a drink. More than once, Hickok was arrested for vagrancy. He was approaching 40, he was losing his signature flowing hair, and, more importantly for a gunfighter, he was losing his vision.

In 1876, Hickok was diagnosed with glaucoma and ophthalmia, which some claimed was contracted as an STD. Today it is believed that Wild Bill actually had trachoma, a common vision problem in the 19th century. The disease was the result of a bacterial infection, common in crowded, dirty living conditions. It still exists today in third world countries, but has been eradicated in the U.S. If left untreated, trachoma can lead to blindness. So can venereal disease, which was another frequent explanation for Hickok's deteriorating vision. Hickok, like many men of his era, was known to frequent brothels and bordellos and may have acquired syphilis, which if untreated could also lead to vision loss.

Whatever the reason, Hickok's gunfighting days were over. Perhaps this made the prospect of marriage enticing to both Wild Bill and Alice, because within a month of reuniting in Cheyenne, they were married there on March 5, 1876. Agnes was 11 years older than her new husband, who lied about his age on his marriage certificate. He said he was 46, but he was really 39. The minister, apparently not feeling optimistic about this union, made a notation in the marriage record: "Don't think they meant it."[2] Following the marriage, the couple honeymooned in Cincinnati for two weeks so that Hickok could meet his in-laws. Agnes stayed in Cincinnati, as Emma was due to give birth at any time, while Hickok took a train back to Cheyenne before joining the gold rush in South Dakota. The next stop for Wild Bill Hickok would be his last stop: Deadwood.

Deadwood and Calamity Jane

Deadwood in the Black Hills of South Dakota was like many mining towns, save for the fact that it was not supposed to be there. The land where George Custer found gold along the French Creek technically belonged to the Lakota-Sioux Indian tribe, since the Black Hills were granted to the Lakota in the Treaty of Laramie in 1868. The government tried to conceal the discovery and, despite the military presence to try and keep out the prospectors, Deadwood became a thriving – and lawless – boomtown. It was difficult to pass laws in a town that legally could not be possessed by the U.S.

---

[2] James McLaird. *Wild Bill Hickok and Calamity Jane: Deadwood Legends.* Chapter 3.

Custer

When Hickok arrived in Deadwood in 1876, he found himself in what might be described as his element, except that it was difficult to say what his element was at this point in his life. He told those that would listen in the saloons that he was going to head out to the hills and look for gold, but he was never the type of man to work for someone else, so that was unlikely. He was most at home at the poker table, which there was plenty of in Deadwood. He wrote several letters to his wife, promising that that they would be together and build a home soon.

Legend has it that Martha Jane Cannary, more famously known as Calamity Jane, was secretly married to Hickok, and when she died her last words were to request that she be buried next to her husband. Some say she claimed to have divorced Wild Bill so that he could marry Agnes. In fact, in 1936, a woman calling herself Jean Hickok McCormick presented herself and a diary she claimed belonged to Martha Jane at a public assistance office in Billings, Montana. Mrs. McCormick said that the diary not only verified her birthday, but also proved that she was the daughter of Wild Bill Hickok and Calamity Jane. CBS Radio believed her and invited her to do a nationally broadcast interview. Apparently, the Billings Office of Public Welfare believed her, too, and gave her the old age assistance that she requested.

Calamity Jane

In reality, Hickok was never married Calamity Jane and they did not have a daughter. It appears that he did not even like her much, although he accepted her presence. Calamity Jane was a big of character as the Wild West ever saw. She was a prostitute at various times in her life, and she was known for dressing in men's clothing and for her taste for alcohol. She could not read or write, swore as much as any man, and lied so much about her life that it was hard to know what was true. Despite this, she was a generally well-liked woman until she wore out her welcome, as was the case when she first met Hickok.

Around June 1876, Hickok was preparing to leave Wyoming and join a wagon train with his friend, Charlie Utter, who had become close with Hickok in the previous years. The trip was not going to be an easy one, as they would be passing through Indian territory to get to the Black Hills. In fact, the same week that they reached Fort Laramie, General Custer was killed at the Little Big Horn River in Montana. The wagon train took the advice they got from the military at Fort Laramie and joined a group of about 30 other wagons headed the same direction. One of the members of this group was Calamity Jane, and the military was anxious to be rid of her. Hickok and Utter were told that she was partially naked in the post guardhouse, where she had been partying with the soldiers who had just received their paychecks. The officer asked if Hickok and Utter's party would take her and they agreed. With no clothes for a woman, they gave her an ill-fitting buckskin outfit and she joined the group, occasionally helping the cook and regaling the crowd of gold-seekers with her stories on the two-week journey to Deadwood.

Calamity Jane also became the mistress of Steve Utter's brother, Charlie, but not Hickok. He could hardly avoid her as she regularly hit him up for a sip out of the five-gallon jug of whiskey that he had brought along for the trip. Unlike Jane, Hickok was quiet much of the trip. When the group reached Custer City, Hickok did not make much of an impression on the town's residents. A journalist from the Black Hills area said many years later that the town viewed him as a bum and thought no better of the women he traveled with. In fact, when the wagon train reached Deadwood, the local newspaper reported not the arrival of Wild Bill Hickok, but Calamity Jane. This was not Jane's first trip into Deadwood, and for a mining town where few women could be found, she was a memorable dance hall girl. Jane did not camp with the men once they arrived into town, but returned for food and later for money to buy new clothes. She was having a hard time supporting herself and competing with the other women in town in her buckskin outfit. The men loaned her the cash, which she repaid with her earnings, presumably as a prostitute, dance hall girl, or both.

Few, if any members of Hickok's group recalled him actually prospecting for gold. He did some target shooting in the woods in the morning and still had enough skill to impress a reporter with his ability to shoot a tomato can out of the air. The reporter, Leander Richardson from *The Springfield Republican* in Massachusetts, confirmed that Calamity Jane was enamored with Charlie Utter, called Colorado Charlie, not Hickok. Like Hickok, Charlie was a snappy dresser, had long blonde hair, and fascinated the locals with his morning ritual of taking a bath, a completely unique habit back then. Utter was also as neat with his surroundings as he was with his appearance and kept a very tidy tent. One night after a drunken binge, Hickok went into Charlie's tent and fell asleep on his bed, which was made with fine linens and a blanket. When Charlie found him, he dragged Hickok out by his feet and deposited him on the ground.

At this point in his life, Hickok was most likely an alcoholic. Before he could begin his day, he needed a drink and could be seen with his hair tied back into a knot, gun shoved into his belt, running toward the saloon to get a stash of liquor to bring back to his tent to help him get dressed and complete his morning routine. He was also addicted to poker, but some suggested that he was out of his league with the professional players in Deadwood.

Deadman's Hand at the Saloon No. 10

The location of Saloon No. 10

Fittingly, the death of Wild Bill Hickok is shrouded in legend and mystery, and it's still not completely clear why he was shot by Broken Nose Jack McCall. It is believed that in a poker game on or around August 1, 1876, Hickok took all of 24 year-old Jack McCall's money. Allegedly, Hickok gave McCall a bit of his money back so that he could eat, but not before scolding McCall for betting more money than he had to lose. This was said to have enraged the young man.

Hickok was in Deadwood on August 2, 1876 to take part in a friendly card game at Saloon No. 10. To show how far Hickok's stock had fallen by the time he got to Deadwood, he found himself sitting with his back to the door, a table position he would never allow himself to take in the old days. Wild Bill had a habit of sitting with his back to a wall so he could see anyone and everyone coming toward him, a habit he had developed when he was making enemies as a marshal. This time, Wild Bill twice asked Charles Rich to change chairs with him, but he was ignored. A decade earlier, Hickok would only have had to direct a man to move, and he would have done so out of fear and/or respect.

It's possible that Hickok wouldn't have stood a chance even with his back to the wall. As the game progressed, nobody paid any attention to Jack McCall, an indication that nobody had any reason to suspect he had a score to settle. As the table was playing 5 card draw, McCall approached Hickok from behind, shouted "Take that!" and fired a shot into the back of Hickok's head, killing him instantly. The shot was so point blank that the bullet exited Hickok's cheek and struck one of the other players, Captain Massie, in the wrist. As Hickok's lifeless body slumped onto the table, his cards fell from his hand, revealing two pair, black Aces and black 8s. Though a full house of Jacks over 10s used to be known back then as the Dead Man's Hand, Hickok's legendary death and hand eclipsed it, and Aces and 8s have been known as Dead Man's Hand since Wild Bill's legend took off. Charlie Utter would claim the body and file a notice in the *Black Hills Pioneer*, ""Died in Deadwood, Black Hills, August 2, 1876, from the effects of a pistol shot, J. B. Hickock (Wild Bill) formerly of Cheyenne, Wyoming. Funeral services will be held at Charlie Utter's Camp, on Thursday afternoon, August 3, 1876, at 3 o'clock P. M. All are respectfully invited to attend."

After stunningly shooting Hickok, McCall backed out of the saloon with his gun raised and made his way to his horse, but the cinch was loose and McCall fell to the ground. He ran for cover in the butcher shop but was discovered by a group of locals. McCall claimed that he shot Hickok in revenge for the death of his own brother in Kansas, but there is no evidence that he had a brother. Some say his feelings were bruised over the remarks Hickok made to him about betting over his head. Whatever the reason, an impromptu trial was held the next day among the local miners in the town. Even though there was no official law enforcement in Deadwood, the citizens tried to maintain some form of order with familiar mechanisms, such as jury trials. Despite overwhelming evidence that McCall killed Hickok in cold blood, he pleaded his case, saying that he was exacting revenge for his brother's death and that Hickok claimed that he would kill him too. Incredibly, McCall was declared innocent and set free, and he promptly left town, no doubt wary of retribution from Hickok's friends. In response to the verdict, the *Black Hills Pioneer* editorialized, "Should it ever be our misfortune to kill a man ... we would simply ask that our trial may take place in some of the mining camps of these hills."

The day after the trial, Charlie Utter arranged for Hickok's funeral. Wild Bill was laid out in a beautiful coffin in a tee-pee, where his friends and the people of Deadwood congregated to pay their last respects to one of the West's most famous icons. The grave marker read, "Wild Bill, J.

B. Hickock killed by the assassin Jack McCall in Deadwood, Black Hills, August 2, 1876. Pard, we will meet again in the happy hunting ground to part no more. Good bye, Colorado Charlie, C. H. Utter."

Steve and Charlie Utter at Wild Bill's grave

McCall refused to simply consider himself lucky to get away with murder. When he made it to Wyoming, he continued to talk about his one claim to fame and bragged about the killing of Wild Bill Hickok. When officials in Wyoming heard about it, they did not accept the verdict from the citizen court in Deadwood. McCall was formally charged and extradited to Yankton, South Dakota. Since Deadwood was not a legal jurisdiction, it was claimed that trying him would not be double jeopardy. Thus McCall stood trial again, and this time he was found guilty. "The coward McCall hanged for the murder of Hickok on March 1, 1877. A reporter in town who claimed to talk to McCall filed a report (almost certainly wrongly) claiming, "As I write the closing lines of this brief sketch, word reaches me that the slayer of Wild Bill has been rearrested by the United State authorities, and after trial has been sentenced to death for willful murder. He is now at Yankton, D.T. awaiting execution. At the trial it was proved that the murderer was hired to do his work by gamblers who feared the time when better citizens should appoint Bill the champion of law and order – a post which he formerly sustained in Kansas border life, with credit to his manhood and his courage."

Chapter 7: Hickok's Legacy

Hickok was buried in Ingleside Cemetery in Deadwood, but the cemetery filled quickly, so three years later Charlie Utter had his remains moved to Mount Moriah Cemetery. Due to vandalism, Hickok's grave marker has changed a few times. A cast iron fence now protects his grave and a monument to him stands nearby.

Wild Bill's grave marker today

Calamity Jane visited Hickok's grave often and some say she was infatuated with him. Three years after Hickok's death, she was remembered for her kindness and compassion in nursing many of the town's citizens when Deadwood was hit by a smallpox epidemic. In 1903, Calamity Jane died and was buried next to Hickok. Some say it was her dying wish, but others say that it was intended as a posthumous joke against Hickok because he wasn't actually fond of her. If Jane did love him, he did not reciprocate her feelings. Most likely, it was a decision made by the town officials to boost tourism.

As for Jean McCormick, she was simply a broke woman who invented an identity and defrauded the Montana government out of a state pension. When she died, she was buried in Billings with a tombstone that reads, "Daughter of Jane 'Calamity Jane' Cannary and James Butler 'Wild Bill' Hickok."

Hickok's widow, Agnes, died in 1907 in New Jersey at her son-in-law's home. She never saw Hickok after their Cincinnati honeymoon and when she died, she was buried next to her first husband.

The Myth of Wild Bill Hickok

James Butler Hickok lived what could be considered an interesting life, but when examined next to that of other men and women of the Wild West, his achievements are far from remarkable. He served the Union well in the Civil War but his careers in law enforcement and acting were relatively short-lived. Certainly his skills as a shooter set him apart from other men, which may have been enough to cultivate his mythical status, but that's hardly something most people would care to be known for outside of the West.

Hickok's image was certainly helped along by J.W. Buel, a journalist from St. Louis who published "The Life and Marvelous Adventures of Wild Bill The Scout," a mixture of fact and sensational fiction that made Hickok out to be a superhero of the West. This theme of Hickok restoring order in the uncivilized West was repeated many times in biographies and dime novels that followed, and these publications especially fed the East Coast's fascination with the frontier. Hickok became such a hero that his family was repeatedly approached after his death for souvenirs. His family, particularly his nephews, also spent a great deal of time trying to dispel myths about him and to tell the truth about his life, especially about his relationship with Calamity Jane.

As time passed, historians began to uncover some of the facts about Hickok, which detracted from his status as a hero. In 1926, the same year that Frank Wilstach published "Wild Bill Hickok, Prince of Pistoleers," attempts to set the record straight about Hickok riled the secretary of the Kansas State Historical Society. Kansas considered Hickok one of its own, and the secretary, William Connelly, would not allow his reputation to be tarnished. Connelly eventually published his own glowing biography, "Wild Bill – James Butler Hickok." Not to be outdone, the State of Illinois raised $10,000 to erect a granite statute to Hickok, which was dedicated at New State Park in his hometown of Troy Grove on August 29, 1929. The plaque reads, in part, "He contributed largely in making the west a safe place for women and children. His sterling courage was always at the service of right and justice."[3]

The Hickok legend made the leap to the silver screen beginning with the silent movie era, and by 2012 Wild Bill had been either a supporting or starring character in no less than 35 films. The first significant film was the 1923 silent movie "Wild Bill Hickok." The original screen cowboy, William S. Hart, who was friends with another real-life Western icon, Wyatt Earp, portrayed him. Hart's version of Hickok had Wild Bill ridding Dodge City of various outlaws and desperadoes. As she would many times, Calamity Jane is featured along with Wild Bill, continuing to give life to the notion that they had a romantic relationship. This did not sit well

---

[3] Joseph G. Rosa. *They Called Him Wild Bill.* Page 3.

with Hickok's family, who were upset that he would be portrayed as having Jane as girlfriend when he was married to Agnes, a woman with a reputation that was quite a bit different from that of Calamity Jane's.

Hart

A year later, legendary director John Ford included tales of Hickok and his pal Buffalo Bill during their adventures on the Pony Express in the sprawling epic "Iron Horse." In 1936, one of the biggest stars in Hollywood, Gary Cooper, portrayed Hickok, who saved the enchanting Calamity Jane, played by Jean Arthur, from the Cheyenne Indians in Cecil B. DeMille's "The Plainsmen." When the film's screenwriter, Jean MacPherson, warned DeMille that trying to claim that Jane was Bill's girlfriend could cause some controversy, she was right. Hickok's family wrote letters to DeMille, who responded that he was simply giving the public what they wanted. Still, he did eventually make some plot changes in deference to the family, particularly nixing the idea of Hickok marrying Jane and riding off into the sunset with her and Buffalo Bill.

In 1938, Columbia presented the movie serial "The Great Adventures of Wild Bill Hickok." Serials were short movies shown prior to the main feature, and this one has Hickok as the marshal of Abilene battling the Phantom Riders, intent on stopping the cattle drives across the Chisholm Trail and stopping the building of a new railroad. Even into 1995, Hickok warranted his own movie when Jeff Bridges played him in "Wild Bill," opposite Ellen Barkin's Calamity Jane.

When television began to take hold of American living rooms and Westerns were all the rage,

Hickok got his own television show. "The Adventures of Wild Bill Hickok," starred Guy Madison as Bill and, in a move that would no doubt cause a reaction from the real Hickok, Andy Devine played his comedic sidekick, the rotund Deputy Marshal Jingles P. Jones. Devine made a catch-phrase out of the saying, "Hey Wild Bill – wait for me!" The series ran from 1951 through 1958 and was nominated for an Emmy in 1955.

The Hickok image has even been evoked by U.S. presidents. On November 23, 1953, President Dwight Eisenhower spoke about his hometown of Abilene, Kansas at a B'nai B'rith Dinner, honoring the 40th anniversary of the Anti-Defamation League. He said:

> "We had as our marshal for a long time a man named Wild Bill Hickok. If you don't know anything about him, read your Westerns more. Now that town had a code, and I was raised as a boy to prize that code. It was: meet anyone face to face with whom you disagree. You could not sneak up on him from behind, or do any damage to him, without suffering the penalty of an outraged citizenry. If you met him face to face and took the same risks he did, you could get away with almost anything, as long as the bullet was in the front.[4]"

30 years later, President Ronald Reagan, who portrayed his share of cowboys as an actor in Hollywood, said at the opening of the Library of Congress's "American Cowboy" exhibit, "Tales of Wild West men and women from Kit Carson to Wild Bill Hickok to Calamity Jane to Annie Oakley are woven into the dreams of our youths and the standards we aim to live by in our adult lives."[5]

Certainly, both presidents paint a romantic notion of both Hickok and the West. However, when thinking about the legacy of Hickok and others of the era in which he lived, it is important to keep their times in context. The America that they lived in – especially the West – was nothing like the modern United States. The West was still untamed territory, and many today still question how and why killers and prostitutes are seemingly held up as examples to live by, but it is important to keep in mind that simply to survive in that era was an achievement. In many respects, the men and women of the West were survivors, made evident by the fact that men even as well known as Wild Bill felt the need to exaggerate their own life stories and come across as even more fearless and deadly than they actually were. To a great extent, that continues to account for the appeal of the Wild West and its legends today.

To many, the legends of the West, including Hickok, continue to represent independence, drive, and initiative, which are all ideals that Americans hold in high esteem. Historians have

---

[4] Joseph G Rosa. *Wild Bill Hickok: The Man and His Myth*. Page 153.
[5] Stanford University: Exploring the West. "Historical Myth v. Reality" http://www.stanford.edu/group/west/cgi-bin/pager.php?id=13

grappled with separating fact from fiction in piecing together the story of James Butler Hickok, which may ultimately prove impossible. Records were not maintained the same way, memories fade, and mementos get lost. However, the facts may not tell the whole story about Hickok. What cannot be denied is his place in American mythology. For many, he continues to represent the best of America's values. He was an independent spirit, something that was instilled in him by his mother and stayed with him throughout his life. America loves heroes and made him one, as well as a true icon of the Wild West.

Bibliography

Fifer, Barbara and Jerry Bryant. *Bad Boys of the Black Hills: And Some Wild Women, Too.* Helena, MT: Farcountry Press. 2008.

McLaird, James. *Wild Bill Hickok and Calamity Jane: Deadwood Legends.* [Kindle version]. Retrieved from Amazon.com. 2008.

Rosa, Joseph G. "George Ward Nichols and the Legend of Wild Bill Hickok." *Arizona and the West, Vol. 19.* 1977

Rosa, Joseph G. *They Called Him Wild Bill.* Norman, OK: University of Oklahoma Press. 1979.

Rosa, Joseph G. *Wild Bill Hickok: The Man and His Myth.* Lawrence, KS: University Press of Kansas. 1996.

Stanford University. "Exploring the West: Historical Myth v. Reality." Retrieved July 25, 2012 from http://www.stanford.edu/group/west/cgi-bin/pager.php?id=13.

Wyatt Earp & Doc Holliday

Chapter 1: Wyatt's Early Years

Childhood Years

Wyatt and his mother

Nicholas Porter Earp was a wanderer. As a young man, he led his family as they crisscrossed the Plains and into the western United States, always in search of the next "big thing" that could put money in his pocket. On July 27, 1840, the widower with one son married Virginia Ann Cooksey in Hartford, Kentucky. They had eight children, including Nick Earp's fourth son, Wyatt Berry Stapp Earp. Wyatt was born on March 19, 1848 in Monmouth, Illinois, and was named for his father's captain in the Mexican-American War. Shortly after he was born, Nick moved the family to a farm in Pella, Iowa, where the family would remain for several years.

Wyatt's boyhood home in Pella

Being the son of Nick Earp could be challenging. He was known to drink to excess, didn't always pay his bills, and could be a bully. His sons were a close-knit group, to the point that Wyatt tried to run away and join his older brothers, Newton, James, and Virgil, when they were fighting for the Union in the Civil War. More than once, Nick found 13 year-old Wyatt and had to bring him back home. Wyatt became a proficient - if unwilling - farmer by the time the Earps pulled up stakes again in 1864, this time to join a wagon train headed to California.

It was in California that the Earps heard the news that Robert E. Lee's Confederate Army of Northern Virginia had surrendered to Ulysses S. Grant and the Army of the Potomac at Appomattox, informally bringing the Civil War to an end. With the end of the war came the true unification of the United States, at least in geography if not in ideals and culture. Considered by many to be the greatest engineering innovation of the 19th century, the Transcontinental Railroad would not only bring people, industry, goods, and ideas west, it would provide Wyatt with work as a young man and expose him to the type of rough and tumble environment that he revisited time and again throughout his life.

Nothing made the Wild West wild more than the railroad. As the Union Pacific forged its way west from Omaha, temporary towns referred to as "Hell on Wheels" popped up in anticipation of the railroad workers. These men worked hard during the day, often in extreme conditions in remote locations. They needed somewhere to spend their money and looked forward to the chance to blow off some steam. Card players, drinkers, prostitutes, and thieves were as much a part of the railroad worker's life as laying track, and young Wyatt saw it all as he graded track for the rail line. His time spent working for the Union Pacific in Wyoming in 1868 taught him two skills that soon became part of the Wyatt Earp legend: boxing and gambling.

19 year old Wyatt

Return to His Family

By 1869, Earp had migrated back across the country and rejoined his family in Lamar, Missouri. Still only 21 years old, he had already lived a nomadic life and now appeared to be settling down. As a young adult, he replaced his father as the town constable when Nick became justice of the peace, and it was Nick who performed the ceremony when Wyatt married Urilla Sutherland, the daughter of a local hotel owner, his father performs the ceremony. With his new wife, Wyatt bought a house on the outskirts of town, and it wasn't long before Urilla was pregnant. With a job, a wife, a house, and a child on the way, Earp's life seemed to be a picture of stability.

The tranquil life of Wyatt Earp lasted less than a year. Within a year, 21 year-old Urilla and her unborn child were dead, for reasons that are still not completely clear. Some later accounts blamed typhoid or complications related to childbirth, but whatever the actual cause of her death, Urilla's brothers blamed Wyatt for their sister's death, leading to a brawl in the streets of Lamar between the Earp brothers and the Sutherland brothers.

Shortly after that incident, with his unsettled life seemingly in shambles, Wyatt sold the house that he had purchased just a few months earlier and left Lamar a changed man.

Chapter 2: Doc's Early Years

When John Henry Holliday was born on August 14, 1851, in Spalding County, Georgia, the Southern Frontier was less than two decades removed from being the land of the Cherokees. His father, Henry Burroughs Holliday, was a self-made man who believed in the Southern codes of honor, independence, and community. As a reward for assisting the First Georgia volunteers in removing the Cherokees and starting them on their Trail of Tears west, Henry Holliday was given 160 acres of land in Pike County.

Henry settled in the town of Griffin, which would later be part of the newly created Spalding County. For a man seeking a life of respectability, he could have not chosen a better wife than Alice Jane McKey of the South Carolina McKeys. Beautiful, fair-haired, and a lover of music, Alice became Henry's wife on January 8, 1849, three months before her 20th birthday. By the time Alice and Henry were expecting their first child, Henry was a respected man in the community, working as a druggist and accumulating land on the side. Martha Eleanora was born on December 3, 1849, but the baby was frail from the start and died half a year later on June 12, 1850.

When John Henry was born a little over a year later, Henry and Alice's grief turned to joy. Not even his cleft palate, which was surgically repaired in a delicate procedure for the times, could dampen their spirits. Their first-born son was a symbol of hope for the future. Henry and Alice never had more children, but their household was often full of extended relatives and even orphans that Henry agreed to care for.

Everything seemed to be falling into place until 1861, when it all changed in the South. Major Holliday joined the Confederate army on October 31, 1861, serving under General P.G.T. Beauregard. In the major's absence, John Henry grew closer to his mother. Alice was determined that her son would be a Southern gentleman, and indeed it was a quality that stayed with him for the rest of his life. When she became sick, John Henry's feelings of protectiveness for his mother only increased.

General Beauregard

In the mid-19th century, tuberculosis was called consumption, a play on the fact that it seemed to eat away at the body until its victims literally drowned when their lungs could no longer function. It was not believed to be contagious, but rather hereditary, and the treatment prescribed to women was usually to stay home and perform their typical domestic duties, which essentially amounted to doing nothing different than perhaps eating a more bland diet. When the major returned to a war-torn Georgia after resigning his commission due to chronic diarrhea, Alice was weak and bedridden. He felt like he had no choice but to move his family as far from the war front as he could while still remaining in Georgia. Thus, in 1864, he moved them to Valdosta.

Once the Holliday family arrived in their new home, John Henry attended the Valdosta Institute for grammar school, receiving rigorous training in rhetoric and the classics from Samuel Varnedoe, a man credited with focusing more on achievement and nurturing of learning than disciplining with a switch. John Henry was a good student, well mannered, and popular with his classmates, and at home he was developing a close relationship with his older cousin, Mattie, whose family had come to Valdosta to join his own. His relationship with Mattie is just one of the great mysteries of his life. Some suggest that their relationship turned to romance, although there was never any confirmation of this. Either way, they did keep in contact throughout his life and he wrote to Mattie often. However, his world was turned upside down when his mother died from consumption on September 16, 1866.

John Henry was furious when 23 year-old neighbor Rachel Martin married his father three months later. To him, as well as to other members of the family, it was disrespectful to his mother's memory, and it was only made worse when Major Holliday moved his family from their farm to a house owned by his new in-laws. Others questioned the circumstances that would call for such a quick marriage. With a lawsuit filed against him by his former brother-in-law, who wanted his deceased sister's property back and questioned Henry's fidelity, Major Holliday's once close-knit family started to unravel.

Congressional candidate J.W. Clift visited the county courthouse to make a campaign speech on April 4, 1868. The courthouse happened to also be the headquarters for the Freedmen's Bureau, which was created in 1865 to assist former slaves with emergency food, shelter, medical care, and in some cases, family reunification. Major Holliday's appointment as an agent for the Freedmen's Bureau upset local citizens, as well as his son. When a small explosion went off during Clift's speech, John Henry was one of the young men suspected of involvement. Whether the young Holliday was actually involved is not known for sure, but it is known that Major Holliday's son was becoming angry and rebellious enough to do it.

John Henry Holliday, D.D.S.

Exactly why John Henry entered dental school is not clear, but chances are that he received some encouragement from his uncle, John Stiles Holliday, a respected physician who was living in Atlanta in 1869. Dr. Holliday was growing disillusioned with medicine and believed that dentistry was more respectable and, in many ways, more progressive. Dentists were already using anesthesia, while most doctors were still skeptical. Licensing standards for doctors were also loose, opening the door for scam artists selling questionable remedies. When Dr. Lucian Frink, a friend of Major Holliday's, agreed to be his preceptor, John Henry paid the $100 tuition and enrolled in Frink's alma mater, the Pennsylvania College of Dental Surgery.

Starting in October 1870, Holliday attended classes six days a week. The Valdosta Institute had prepared him well for the rigors of dental school. Chartered in 1856, the Pennsylvania College of Dental Surgery was one of the largest and most prestigious dental colleges in the world at the time, and in addition to attending lectures on topics such as chemistry, anatomy, and dental pathology, Holliday worked at the school's free clinic, which had developed an outstanding reputation for its dental care.

Holliday had never left Georgia before and, no doubt, Philadelphia was a new world for a young man who had been born and bred in the South. Holliday obviously went on to spend much of his life as a drinker and a gambler, and it would not be out of the realm of possibilities that he got his first exposure to these elements in Philadelphia. Still, Holliday was a good student. In March 1871, he returned to Valdosta to continue his training under Frink before going back to Philadelphia in September to complete his second year of studies. After writing his master's thesis, "Diseases of the Teeth," Holliday and 25 of his classmates attended graduation ceremonies and received their Doctor of Dental Surgery degrees.

It would be another five months before Holliday would receive his license to practice dentistry, because Georgia state law required that he be 21 years old and he was still only 20. In the meantime, he worked as an assistant to one of his classmates, A. Jameson Fuches, Jr., who opened a practice in St. Louis, Missouri.

The raucous river city offered Holliday more than professional experience. St. Louis was the home of a foster care runaway whose given name was Mary Katharine Harony. Born in Hungary, she had come to the U.S. and went by the name Kate Fisher, but in Western lore, she became best known by her nickname Big Nose Kate. Like many women of her time who had no family, she became a prostitute, and in 1872 she was living in a brothel and worked at a saloon not far from Dr. Fuches's office on Fourth Street.

Big Nose Kate (left) in 1865

Whether she started out as his girlfriend or he initially paid for her company, Kate and John Henry began their often-stormy relationship in St. Louis. Perhaps he was attracted to her courage, but her distrust of other people, especially of Wyatt Earp, would be a source of conflict in their relationship throughout much of Holliday's life. There is no evidence to support Kate's claim that they were married in Valdosta in 1876, but it is a fact that even though Holliday left St Louis without her in July 1872, it was far from the end of his time with Fisher.

Big Nose Kate, circa 1890

Holliday returned to Georgia just before his 21st birthday to claim the inheritance from his mother and then moved in with John Stiles Holliday in Atlanta, who by now had given up his medical practice for the grocery business. He renewed his friendship with his cousin, Robert, or Hub as he was known in the family, and the two handsome bachelors quickly established themselves in the Atlanta social scene. Hub would go on to become an esteemed dentist, graduating from the same school as John Henry, and he later helped found a dental college in Atlanta that was incorporated into Emory University in 1944.

John Stiles Holliday helped introduce his nephew to friends and associates in Atlanta with a party in the ballroom of his home and gave him a revolver just like the one he had given his three sons, an 1851 Colt revolver. The Holliday household in Atlanta also included Sophie Walton, the family's biracial servant. An expert card player who was adept with numbers, Sophie helped John Henry in his education as a gambler, providing information that would prove useful in the years that he would spend as a player and a dealer in the game of choice, faro. In the 19th century, Faro became one of the most popular gambling games in the U.S., especially in the West, where it was often called "Bucking the Tiger" because of the backs of early cards that featured a drawing of a Bengal Tiger.

Samuel Hape was also living with the Hollidays at that time. He had founded Atlanta Dental in 1868, and during the Civil War Hape was the only source of dental supplies for the Confederacy. He was acquainted with the dentist Arthur C. Ford and arranged for John Henry to have an interview with Dr. Ford. On July 26, 1872, Ford took out a notice in *The Atlanta Constitution* saying that Dr. John Holliday would be covering for him during his absence at a conference in August. Since Dr. Ford frequently had to travel, John Henry filled in for him on a regular basis.

Soon, John Henry became a landowner, assuming ownership of a building in Griffin that had belonged to his mother's family. When Hub had decided to quit dental school, thinking it was no longer necessary, John Henry talked him out of it and agreed to be Hub's preceptor at his alma mater. John Stiles promised financial assistance for the two young men to set up their practice together. Everything was aligning for John Henry Holliday to be a dentist and a respected member of Atlanta society.

Chapter 3: Wyatt Earp, Law Enforcer

Any thoughts Earp may have had about leading a stable, quite life in Missouri disappeared after the death of his wife and unborn child. Had he remained in Lamar, he would have needed to answer to lawsuits filed against him for misdeeds as town constable, including misusing funds. However, it did not take long for Earp to find more trouble as he headed back west. He was arrested in Van Buren, Arkansas in 1871 for stealing horses in Indian Territory but didn't stick around long enough for the trial, instead climbing out of the top of his jail cell and heading back to Illinois.

Finding himself on the run yet again, Earp traveled back west across the frontier, which by now was dotted with small cities and towns that had attracted the "Hell on Wheels" types. While all of the shady types posed problems for local law enforcement, Earp immersed himself in these cities, becoming notorious for being a regular patron of the saloons, gambling halls, and brothels that were in whatever town he had taken up temporary residence. That the young man would eventually become the West's most iconic figure would've made contemporaries of this time laugh, as they most often saw him in the company of prostitutes. At one point, he lived in a small, damp room on a floating brothel on the Illinois River, and it has even been suggested that Earp was a pimp, though whether or not this was true is not known for certain. Regardless, it is known that he was arrested several times for his involvement with prostitutes, and one working prostitute referred to herself as his wife for a period of time. Therefore, it should have surprised nobody when he eventually made his way to Kansas, where his brother, James, opened a brothel of his own.

James Earp

Earp had no trouble finding work in the raucous cattle town of Wichita during the summer. When cattle drivers came into town, the brothels of Wichita were busy, and Earp's skills as a bouncer came in handy when order needed to be restored. However, Earp found himself with little work to do in October 1874, so he accepted a job helping an off-duty Wichita policeman track down a wagon thief. After successfully locating the thieves and retrieving the stolen property, a positive article in the *Wichita Eagle* changed Earp's reputation. He was now publicly praised for a change, instead of being sued, chased, or otherwise vilified.

Buoyed by the positive press, Earp agreed to be a deputy marshal during summers in Wichita and later, in Dodge City. Unusually big for men of his era at 6 feet and 175 pounds, his physically intimidating methods were useful in dealing with the Texas cowboys who were in Dodge City to unwind. Though he would later become legendary for his deadly aim, Earp was proficient enough with his fists, and he learned on the job he did not need to fire a weapon to keep some type of order among the chaos. He was an efficient deputy and became a respected lawman in Kansas, often doing his work without even carrying a gun. In one of the times he did carry a gun, he inadvertently dropped it while leaning back in a chair, causing it to fire when it hit the ground and send a bullet through his coat. It may have been the first bullet to graze Earp's clothes, but it certainly wouldn't be the last.

Wyatt had rehabilitated his image and seemed to be finding a successful calling, but Marshal Earp was still courting controversy. During Wichita's election for city marshal on April 2, 1876, a former marshal accused Earp of using his office's powers to hire his brothers, a charge that led to Earp punching him out and publicly beating him. As a result, Wichita's lawman was arrested for disturbing the peace, bringing his stint as Marshal in Wichita to an abrupt end.

Chapter 4: Wyatt Earp and Doc Holliday Head West

Earp's Path to Tombstone

Wyatt's time in Wichita was over, but his career as a lawman certainly wasn't, and he didn't have to go far to find his next job. By 1876, Dodge City, Kansas had become a popular destination spot for cattle drives starting from as far south as Texas. It's known that Wyatt was appointed an assistant Marshal in Dodge City, but it's unclear how much time he spent there. It has been widely theorized that Earp even spent some time in the legendary frontier boomtown of Deadwood in the Black Hills of South Dakota, which is as popular as ever today thanks to the shooting of Wild Bill Hicock and a critically acclaimed HBO show about the town. It's also known that Wyatt spent some time in 1877 gambling down in Texas, and it was there that he met a man who would forever be associated with him, John Henry "Doc" Holliday.

Whatever the case, Earp made several famous acquaintances during his time in Dodge City, including with lawman Bat Masterson and prostitute Mattie Blaylock, who became his companion for several years. And on July 26, 1878, Earp was involved in his first famous shooting, which took place in the early morning after cowboy George Hoyt and a few other heavily intoxicated men shot their guns as they headed out of town on horseback. Earp, another policeman named James Masterson, and an untold number of citizens took aim at Hoyt and the others, and as the riders were crossing a bridge, Hoyt was shot in the arm, causing a wound that later developed into gangrene and killed him. Though it's not known who shot Hoyt, Wyatt was all too happy to take the credit, later claiming he fired the shot that hit him.

Mattie Blaylock

By the time of the Hoyt shooting, Wyatt Earp was 30, and though he was still in good standing as an assistant marshal in Dodge City, he wanted something different for his life. He had witnessed the power of wealth each time cattle barons ended their cattle drives in Dodge City, and now he hoped to be able to trade in his badge for the opportunity to make some cash. Wyatt sensed the opportunity had come when his older brother Virgil contacted him about a silver strike in the rugged hills of southern Arizona Territory. Virgil Earp had been living in northern Arizona, serving in various law enforcement roles in the capital of Prescott, and when Virgil was appointed U.S. deputy marshal of Pima County in southern Arizona, he sent for his brothers, Wyatt and Morgan, to serve as special deputies to help him deal with the cowboys. With the lure of striking it rich in the silver mines, Wyatt Earp and Mattie Blaylock left Kansas in 1879 for the silver-mining boomtown of Tombstone, Arizona.

Virgil Earp

Doc Heads to Texas

Dr. Arthur Ford was not a well man. Like Holliday's mother, Dr. Ford was also suffering from consumption, and by New Year's Day 1873, Ford announced that he was going to Florida to recuperate. He turned his practice over to Dr. J. Cooper, not Holliday. Holliday had endured a difficult Christmas. His uncle (Mattie's father), Robert Holliday, died on Christmas Eve, and John Henry was with his family at the funeral. Weeks later, Francisco E'Dalgo, a Mexican orphan that lived with John Henry as a child, died from consumption. The next day, Holliday sold his half of the building he inherited from his mother in Griffin, pocketing $1,800. By the summer, he was in Dallas, Texas.

Why Holliday left Georgia for Dallas is another mystery and subject to much speculation. The most common theory is that he went west for his health. Bouts of coughing that got progressively worse into the winter of 1872 led to confirmation that Holliday, too, had consumption. There was no cure, nor was there really an effective treatment. Some said that Holliday was told to go west where the air is drier and, presumably, easier on his lungs. If there is a flaw to this theory, it is that Dallas can be quite humid and the weather is not that much different from Atlanta. If Holliday truly wanted to seek out dry air, he could have proceeded directly to the desert of the Southwest.

Another theory for his departure is that he was in love with his cousin, Mattie. It was not unheard of for first cousins to marry at the time, but Mattie was Catholic and her religion did not permit it. Certainly, they had a special relationship, but nobody would confirm that their relationship had ever turned to romance. Mattie burned some of the letters he wrote to her and another family member burned the rest of them years later. When he began to transform from Dr.

Holliday, the dentist, into Doc Holliday, the gunman, he still wrote to her even though by that time she was a nun.

A third theory, repeated by lawman turned journalist Bat Masterson, is that Holliday had committed murder and was forced to leave town. Few people deny that Holliday was involved in a shooting incident at swimming hole on the Withlacooche River near Valdosta. His uncle Tom McKey owned land near the river, and members of the family claimed a nearby swimming hole as their own. The African Americans who swam there had been advised to swim elsewhere. One day, a group of white men that included Holliday saw some young African Americans swimming there, despite previous warnings. Some say Holliday drew his Colt and shot over their heads, while others say he killed one, possibly three people. According to Masterson, Holliday said that his family advised him to go away for a while and helped him get to Dallas. Like other similar stories about Holliday, there is no documented evidence or record of the shooting, but that was not at all unusual for this period of history either. White violence against African Americans routinely occurred and went unreported, and it is also not unlikely that family members would sanitize the story, just as they might burn incriminating letters.

Whatever the cause, and perhaps it was a combination of all three theories, John Henry Holliday left his home state and headed west.

Bat Masterson

Dallas was not simply a random location to Holliday. He was acquainted with another dentist, Dr. John A. Seeger and became his partner in his practice in the summer of 1873. Seeger, a non-drinker, was probably pleased if Holliday's claim that he not only stopped drinking but also joined the local temperance society was true. Business was good for the young dentists, but once again, the partnership did not last long and ended the following March. Holliday's taste for whiskey and gambling had resurfaced, as did his illness. Indeed, the correlation between the desire for alcohol and the increasing coughing fits may have gone hand-in-hand.

Holliday was arrested in April 1874 for operating a keno game, but since he paid his property taxes on June 1, it appeared that he was still going to try and stay in Dallas. However, he left for Denison, an edgier, rougher town than Dallas, before the month was over, and it can be safely assumed that dentistry was taking a backseat to the allure of the gaming tables by now. Of course, Holliday may have been left with little choice; it is difficult to imagine that many people wanted a dentist with a persistent cough to treat them.

Regardless of how and why Holliday came to Denison, Holliday was starting to develop a reputation as a dangerous man, though the fact that so many of the stories about him are not supported by witnesses or documentation raises some questions. Certainly, it is not unusual if crimes in a more lawless time go unreported or if records were lost, but some historians have begun to question if Holliday spread the rumors about himself. The reasons may have simply been rooted in self-protection for a man, typically carrying a lot of cash, who often traveled alone through treacherous territory. Others believed that Holliday simply felt that he had little to lose because he knew he would not have a long life, even though he did look for treatment for his condition more than once.

Between 1875 and 1877, Holliday roamed across the West, and wherever he went, stories about shootings and other mayhem followed him. Known now as "Doc," but perhaps using the alias of Tom McKey, there were reports of him killing a solider in Jacksboro, Texas and cutting a man's face in Denver, Colorado. Some say he joined the goldrush in Deadwood, South Dakota, while still other reports placed him in Cheyenne, Wyoming before heading back to Texas. Wyatt Earp claims that Holliday was in Fort Griffin, Texas with Kate Fisher in 1877. Earp was there because he was on the trail of a band of outlaws known as The Trio. He never caught up with them – Bat Masterson eventually arrested them in Kansas in 1878 – but Earp did strike up a friendship with Holliday that became part of both men's legends.

Wyatt and Doc's Friendship

To a great extent, the lives of Doc Holliday and Wyatt Earp will forever be defined by a 30-second gun battle in Tombstone, Arizona, which Earp would spend his final years trying to forget. Holliday was there, too, even though Earp told him he didn't need to be. In fact, no stories about Earp in Tombstone are complete without Holliday. However, Holliday has come to be viewed by many as Earp's sidekick, which is not accurate. Masterson wrote of Holliday in "Human Life" magazine in 1907, "His whole heart and soul were wrapped up in Wyatt Earp…"[6] Holliday was a good friend to Earp and raised to be loyal to his friends, but he was nobody's sidekick.

They met in a saloon in Fort Griffin, but their friendship took hold in Dodge City, Kansas. Upon leaving Texas, Holliday wrote to Mattie in 1878 that he had "enjoyed as much of this as [I] could stand."[7] Earp, as tall as Holliday but much more physically intimidating, aspired to make some cash more than he aspired to be a lawman. Still, he was respected as deputy marshal of Dodge City, which needed a man like Earp to help keep order when the Texas cowboys were in town to blow off steam.

By 1876, Dodge City, Kansas had become a popular destination spot for cattle drives starting from as far south as Texas, and though it's known that Wyatt was appointed an assistant Marshal in Dodge City, but it's unclear how much time he spent there. It has been widely theorized that Earp even spent some time in the legendary frontier boomtown of Deadwood in the Black Hills of South Dakota, which is as popular as ever today thanks to the shooting of Wild Bill Hicock and a critically acclaimed HBO show about the town. It's also known that Wyatt spent some time in 1877 gambling down in Texas, which is where he first met Holliday.

Masterson was the sheriff when Holliday arrived and claimed to tolerate Holliday and his stories more out of respect for Earp than for any good feelings about Doc. Masterson thought that Holliday was dangerous and perhaps a little crazy. When Masterson became a writer, he wrote about Holliday, "He was selfish and had a perverse nature – traits not calculated to make a man popular in the early days of the frontier."[8]

Clearly, Holliday's reputation had preceded him before he arrived in Dodge City, and according to Earp, Holliday's departure from Fort Griffin was hastened by an incident at a poker game involving a man named Ed Bailey. Holliday reportedly advised Bailey to stop playing with the pile of discarded cards, called deadwood, and focus more on the game, which was a way of politely asking him to stop cheating. When Bailey continued to cheat, Holliday whipped out a knife that he always carried and stabbed the man. When Holliday took off to his room, Kate deliberately set a shed on fire to create a diversion and the two escaped to Kansas. Whether the incident really happened the way Earp, who was not a witness, told it or whether it even happened in Texas, nobody knows, but it did contribute to Holliday's reputation as a man who would kill you before he backed down.

---

[6] "Bat Masterson Not Impressed by Doc Holliday." *Territorial News*. December 15, 2010.
[7] Gary L. Roberts. *Doc Holliday: The Life and Legend*. Page 89.
[8] *Territorial News*

Earp also claimed that it was this streak in Holliday that saved Earp's life in 1878 and cemented their friendship. Earp said that he found himself surrounded by outlaws somewhere near the Long Branch Saloon on Dodge City's famous Front Street. Holliday was nearby at a gaming table and saw the men closing in on Earp. After asking the card dealer if he could borrow his six-shooter, Holliday bolted for the door, drew both his own gun and the borrowed gun, and ordered the outlaws to put up their hands. Earp said this gave him time to draw his own gun and place the men under arrest.

Doc Heads to Las Vegas, New Mexico

Initially, at least, Holliday felt a sense of acceptance in Dodge City that eluded him in Texas. Certainly the environment in the dusty cowtown suited him, with enough saloons and faro tables to keep him entertained. The very existence of Dodge City, located in western Kansas, was tied to the state Holliday had left behind. Wealthy cattle barons from Texas passed through and, in many cases, left both their cattle and their cash in Dodge City. The more saloons, brothels, and gaming tables there were, the more opportunity there was for the businessmen of Dodge City to make a profit.

One thing that Dodge City did not have when Holliday arrived was a dentist, prompting him to take out an advertisement in *The Dodge City Times* on June 8, 1878. He offered his dentistry services to the community, with a money-back guarantee. His office was located in Room 24 at the Dodge House Hotel, adjacent to a billiards hall. Holliday even had a pocket dental kit, complete with the basic dental tools of the day, and an inscription with his name and the address of his office. All of this suggests that Holliday might have considered settling down in Kansas.

As it turned out, Holliday did not settle down. He was more successful as a gambler than a dentist, and the dust of Dodge City did little to help his health. His cough was deep and persistent, while his voice had become hoarse due to ulcers in his throat, which often made it hard for him to speak above a whisper. He lost more weight and his color alternated between red and pale. The humidity of Kansas was also no help, but there was word that the Montezuma Hot Springs in Gallinas Canyon in New Mexico had helped others suffering from consumption.

The timing was right to move on if Holliday desired to do so. Dodge City's prime cattle running season was coming to an end with winter just around the corner. The town was also trying to get a handle on prostitution and gambling, and on August 6, 1878 it passed ordinances outlawing both. They were not truly outlawed as the town wanted to regulate the big moneymakers, not eliminate them, but the result was making it more expensive and difficult for a man like Holliday to gamble. Holliday also claimed to be falsely implicated in a robbery at a local store, so with these factors in mind, he and Kate moved on to Las Vegas, New Mexico in the winter of 1878.

They made it as far as Trinidad, Colorado when the snow began to fall. With Doc's health failing, the faced a difficult decision. They either stayed in brutally cold Trinidad or risked Holliday deteriorating even more on the road. Ultimately, they hired a teamster who was on his way to Santa Fe to transport Kate and a very ill Doc to Las Vegas by rail. Doc and Kate arrived in Las Vegas just before Christmas 1878, referring to themselves as Dr. and Mrs. J.H. Holliday. It may have been simply easier to explain their relationship this way even if Kate was just his common-law wife. Northwest of the town plaza was the mecca for consumption patients, 22 springs at the base of the mountains that produced water ranging in temperatures from 110 degrees up to 140 degrees. Las Vegas was full of people, most young and mostly wealthy, who had come to these springs, hoping for a cure for their consumption. They called themselves the Lungers Club.

After settling in, Holliday opened a dental practice in an office not far from the town plaza. He shared space with jeweler and watchmaker, William Leonard, another young man afflicted with consumption. Holliday, already well-acquainted with men with questionable pasts, was not put off by the story that Leonard shot Jose Mares the previous fall in front of a local store and then took a beating from Mares' friends. They developed a friendship that lasted until Leonard was indicted on charges and left town.

Holliday began to recover his strength in Las Vegas and soon felt well enough to open a saloon. However, neither the record-breaking frigid temperatures nor the new law that would prohibit gambling within New Mexico Territory would help Holliday's income as dentist or a saloonkeeper/gambler. He was fined $25 for running a monte table in March 1879, prompting him to head back to Dodge City, this time without Kate. Holliday made a little money there helping Masterson organize a group of fighters for the Atchison, Topeka, & Santa Fe Railroad. The railroad had asked Sheriff Masterson to help fight off attacks on workers in a contested pass at Canon City, Colorado. Holliday did a bit more work for the railroad before he went back to Las Vegas.

By this time, Las Vegas was preparing for the arrival of the railroad, which ultimately bypassed the town by about a mile. Still, businesses were being built, plans were being made and many of the gamblers that Holliday knew from Dodge City followed the line into town. Trouble followed him, too. He was accused of shooting a man named Mike Gordon, who opened gunfire when one of the saloon girls turned down his advances. There were reports of other trouble, too, but like many of the tales about Holliday, it is not known if they ever occurred.

Holliday may have wanted to stay in Las Vegas, but he was soon on the road again. Wyatt Earp and his common-law wife, Mattie, had come to town, talking about a silver strike in Arizona. With the lure of striking it rich in the silver mines, Wyatt Earp and Mattie Blaylock left Kansas in 1879 for the silver-mining boomtown of Tombstone, Arizona. After a stop in Albuquerque, Holliday headed west again, this time for Arizona.

Chapter 5: Becoming Legends in Arizona

Wyatt Strikes Out

Tombstone in 1881

While Wyatt Earp was deputy marshal of Dodge City in 1877, Ed Schieffelin was working for the U.S. government as an Indian scout in Arizona. After leaving the Grand Canyon area, Schieffelin moved south and was stationed at Fort Huachuca, not far from the Mexican border. As he was known to do, Schieffelin went out on his own to search for "rocks." Other soldiers in the camp told him that the only stone he would find out in the rugged hills was his tombstone. When he found silver, the soon-to-be millionaire named his first mine "The Tombstone."

Schieffelin

As word of Schieffelin's discovery spread, prospectors streamed into the camp near where he had staked his claim. The tents soon gave way to buildings, and when the national census was taken in 1880, Tombstone had 2,100 residents. By the time a special census was taken in Arizona in 1882 to accounting for the new counties that had sprung up in the past two years, Tombstone reported 5,300 residents, second only to Tucson. At its peak, as many as 15,000 people crowded Tombstone's dusty streets.

Few, if any, people paid attention to the wagon that carried Earp and Mattie into town in December 1879. Only a few hundred people lived there at the time the Earp family arrived to join Virgil, but the signs of growing wealth were there. Soon there would be churches, restaurants, and shops, some of which were even indicative of the sophistication of the Victorian Era. These symbols of the times often stood in stark contrast to the dusty mines nearby. The Earps had come to Tombstone to cash in like everybody else, but even at this time, Tombstone was quickly becoming the domain of more sophisticated mining companies from cities such as New York, San Francisco, or London. Little was left to small, individual prospectors, even as the town's population exploded over the next several years, and any hopes of getting rich off of the silver mines were short-lived.

Wyatt Earp's rather short retirement from law enforcement ended when he accepted a job as shotgun rider for Wells Fargo. His job was to protect the content of the strongbox under the driver's seat. Weighing up to 150 pounds and made of oak, pine, and iron, the strongboxes containing gold, cash, and other valuables were natural targets for thieves. Earp was glad to leave the job in the summer of 1880, and with his other business ventures having already failed so quickly, he became a deputy sheriff of Tombstone. As was the case in Kansas, Earp was good at his work, a fact that was appreciated by the people of Tombstone. Being in law enforcement in Tombstone was made more challenging, though, by the fact that the authorities in Arizona paid little attention to what the local cowboys did in Mexico.

Doc Heads to Tombstone

Prescott, Arizona bore little resemblance to Tombstone. The northern Arizona town was the capital, lost the title to Tucson in 1867, then got it back again in 1877 before losing it for good to Phoenix in 1889. As the capital city, it was busy and had its share of gambling halls and saloons along famed Whiskey Row. However, it was not a boomtown and lacked the edginess of Tombstone.

Earp had invited Holliday to join him in Tombstone, which stayed in Holliday's mind as he gambled and walked the streets of Prescott. They had arrived in Prescott together in November 1879 and immediately went to see Virgil and Allie Earp, who had been Prescott residents for two years when they told Wyatt about the silver strike. When Jim, Virgil, and Wyatt Earp and their families were ready to go to Tombstone about a week later, where they planned to meet their brother, Morgan, Holliday had already found the gambling scene in Prescott to his liking. He was on a hot streak, so he and Kate opted to stay. This suited Kate just fine as she never really liked Wyatt and did not want Doc to be around him, either.

Kate and Doc's relationship was littered with turbulent periods resulting in frequent separations. One of those periods appears to have come at some point in their stay in Prescott because the 1880 census listed Holliday as a single man. One of his roommates at the boarding house where he lived was John J. Gosper, who happened to be the acting governor of Arizona in General John C. Fremont's absence. No doubt Holliday and Gosper had interesting discussions on the point of alcohol, considering that Gosper was an active member of the temperance society and Holliday was an active indulger of whiskey. Soon, though, Holliday would be on the move again.

Whether it was due to the end of his hot streak at the tables or due to strong recruitment effort by Wyatt, it was September 1880 when Holliday finally arrived in Tombstone, according to voter registration records. Kate, irritated at Doc for reuniting with the Earps, went to Globe, Arizona instead.

When Holliday arrived, Tombstone was still rough around the edges, but it was still also quite a bit different than the town that the Earps rolled into the previous December. Prospector tents from miners looking for the motherlode had given way to permanent buildings and the census shot up from a few hundred when the Earps arrived to 2,100 in 1880. A special census in Arizona in 1882, made necessary by the new counties that were created over the previous two years, indicated that Tombstone's population had grown to 5,300. At one point, it would swell to 15,000 people.

It did not take long for the town to be invaded by wealthy businessmen and entrepreneurs. Their wives could be seen dressed in their finest Victorian dresses, walking along the dusty sidewalks or playing lawn tennis at posh hotels that butted up against the town's dirty mines. Any hopes of individual prospectors, such as the Earps, cashing in were quickly dashed when larger, better financed mining companies from the likes of New York and San Francisco moved into town to strip the mountains of their silver.

Businessmen weren't the only ones making their way to Tombstone. Though cowboys have been historically associated with courage and heroism, to call someone a cowboy at this time was an insult. Ranching and herding were legitimate professions, but a cowboy was a thief. Given its proximity to the border, Tombstone attracted its share of cowboys, who went into Mexico to steal cattle (often murdering innocent Mexicans in the process) and then brought the cattle to Tombstone to sell them to legitimate ranchers. This did not sit well with the businesses that owned the mines. The corporate - and largely Republican - establishment that had come to Tombstone to make money wanted the Earps to keep order. Arizona was still a territory and could not expect to achieve statehood, nor could the corporations expect to attract investors, if chaos and lawlessness reigned. Thus, despite hoping to leave law enforcement behind, Wyatt soon found himself needing work, and by the summer of 1880, he was deputy sheriff in Tombstone.

The Oriental Saloon

The Oriental Saloon was not only the most luxurious saloon and gambling hall in Tombstone, it was one of the finest in the entire West, making it a natural place for Holliday to frequent. On July 22, 1880, The Tombstone Daily Epitaph reported about the Saloon:

"Last evening the portals were thrown open and the public permitted to gaze upon the most elegantly furnished saloon this side of the Golden Gate. Twenty-eight burners suspended in neat chandeliers afforded an illumination of ample brilliancy and the bright rays reflected from the many colored crystals in the bar sparkled like a December icing in the sunshine. The saloon comprises two apartments. To the right of the main entrance is the bar, beautifully carved, finished in white and gilt and capped with a handsomely polished top. In the rear of this stand a brace of sideboards....They were made for the Baldwin Hotel, of San Francisco....The back apartment is covered with a brilliant body brussels [sic] carpet and suitably furnished after the style of a grand club room, with conveniences for the wily dealers in polished ivory....Tombstone has taken the lead and [to] Messrs. Joyce and Co. our congratulations."

When Holliday arrived, the town was experiencing a gambling war between the so-called Easterners, gamblers who came from east of the Pacific Coast, and the Slopers, mostly from California. Wyatt had recently been given an interest in the Oriental's gambling hall, providing him with a cut of the concessions in exchange for helping keep order among the gamblers who hoped to disrupt the town's gambling arrangements.

One of the men doing the disrupting was John E. Tyler from Jackson County, Missouri. Tyler got into trouble in Tombstone on September 23, 1880 when he got into an argument with a gambler associated with the Easterners, but others jumped in and defused the situation before it got out of hand. On October 10, it was Holliday's turn to tussle with Tyler. The two men, unarmed due to the city ordinance against carrying a concealed weapon, got into an argument. Milton Joyce, who leased the bar and was the saloonkeeper that night, helped separate the two men and ordered them to leave. Tyler left, but Holliday began to argue with Joyce. With little effort, Joyce, a much larger man than Holliday, physically removed him from the bar and deposited him into the street.

Joyce

Holliday's pistol had been checked behind the bar and when he walked back into the Oriental to ask for it, Joyce refused. Undeterred, Holliday went to his room at Fly's boardinghouse, got another pistol and went back to the Oriental with his gun drawn. Joyce came out from behind the bar with a gun and may have shot it once, but definitely used it to give Holliday a beating, prompting many to think that Holliday was surely going to die. Shots were fired from all corners by this point and one hit Joyce in the hand. When it was obvious Doc's wounds were not critical, Holliday was arrested and paid a $30 fine. The incident was not over, though, and neither was the feud. The following May, he was indicted by the Grand Jury and after a continuance, a trial was scheduled for October 6, 1881. Holliday would never appear for the trial.

For a time after that, Holliday managed to stay out of legal trouble, focusing his interests on mining properties, acquiring water rights, and, of course, gambling. Kate visited him more than once to try to persuade him to return to Globe with her, where she had opened a hotel. Still harboring bad feelings for the Earps, she no doubt made her feelings known because on at least one occasion, their argument resulted in Doc getting arrested. Her attempts to separate Doc from the Earps only served to drive a wedge in her own relationship with him.

Wyatt's Early Law Enforcement Career in Tombstone

The Earps, by virtue of their role as enforcers for the Republican establishment, were never truly accepted by the community of Democratic ranchers. They were respected for their role, but they were still widely viewed as outsiders. Wyatt's tendency to frequent saloons and gambling halls also raised some eyebrows, as did his friendship with Holliday.

Perhaps not surprisingly, Wyatt quickly found himself caught up in adventure, and controversy, on the job. On October 28, 1880, Tombstone marshal Fred White headed to Allen Street to break up a group of intoxicated men shooting their guns into the air, apparently at the Moon. As White grabbed the pistol of an outlaw cowboy named Curly Bill Brocius, it went off, hitting White in the groin. Wyatt, seeing the start of the confrontation, commandeered someone's pistol and pistol-whipped Curly Bill, all while Curly Bill's friends started shooting at him. White died days later, and even though the Earps likely saved Curly Bill's life by taking him into custody before the mob got hold of him, he remained permanently bitter about being pistol-whipped, and he was implicated by at least one person in the murder of Morgan Earp in March 1882. Curly Bill had become Arizona's most famous outlaw after the shooting of White, but his reign would be short. Less than two years later, Curly Bill would die in a shootout at the hands of none other than Wyatt Earp.

Curly Bill

When the news came from Prescott in Spring 1881 that Tombstone was going to be the seat of Cochise County, Wyatt liked his chances at being named sheriff, which was also a profitable position because the sheriff collected the taxes (and Wyatt already had a history of "misusing" funds and having others go missing). He assumed that being from the North would carry some weight with the Republican governor, John C. Fremont, as would the fact that he was more aligned with the town's business interests, but when it became obvious to Earp that Fremont planned to appoint Democrat Johnny Behan, he withdrew from consideration. Earp also claimed that Behan promised to make him the undersheriff, but this never happened.

Behan

The rivalry for sheriff was not the only thing that Earp and Behan shared. Both men were interested in the affections of 18 year old Josephine "Sadie" Marcus, even though Earp was still involved with Mattie Blaylock. It seems as though Earp was on his way to losing this battle too, at least until Josephine caught Behan in bed with another woman in 1881. Eventually, Earp and Josephine developed their own romance, as Mattie Blaylock descended into drug addiction.

Sadie

The Origins of the Feud with the Clantons and McLaurys

The situation between Earp and Behan did not improve when a Wells Fargo stagecoach on its way to Tombstone from Benson, Arizona was robbed on March 15, 1881. The robbers got away with $26,000, and the driver and a passenger were murdered. Holliday's troubles with Milt Joyce, as well as his trouble with Kate, resurfaced when Kate went back to Tombstone in July. Once again, Kate and Doc argued and Kate turned to alcohol to console herself. Behan and Joyce came across Kate in her drunken condition and suggested a way for her to get back at it Holliday. She swore an affidavit saying that Doc had committed the robbery in Benson. She later said, "I became desperate and in a vain hope of breaking up their [the Earps] association with Doc, whom I loved…I had known I was taking a desperate chance, and I was not astonished when I lost out."[9]

Behan arrested Holliday on July 5, but the case was dropped on July 9. Not a shred of evidence existed to implicate Holliday, but the incident stayed in the minds of many. As for Kate, Doc sent her on her way back to Globe. Meanwhile, the actual killers had yet to be caught and Wells Fargo was unhappy. The company personally insured all cargo and needed to regain the trust of its customers. They wanted the bandits, dead or alive, and they wanted an example made of them. Sheriff Behan organized one posse and Virgil organized another, which included Holliday, Wyatt, and Masterson. Virgil Earp's posse tracked down a man who admitted to holding horses while the robbery occurred and they turned the man over to Behan. The man later escaped from jail, but the Earps claimed that Behan let him go.

---

[9] Reynolds, 155.

Wyatt Earp still had his mind set on getting the sheriff's office and thought that the stagecoach robbery could help, albeit indirectly. He worked out a deal with Ike Clanton, who was well acquainted with the cowboys that made their way in and out of Tombstone. Earp was confident that the cowboys knew who pulled off the robbery and if he could get enough information and solve the case, it seemed like he could score enough political points to become sheriff. Earp offered Clanton $6,000 for his help, which Clanton could not turn down. However, his only condition was that Earp keep the deal a secret. He knew if the cowboys found out about his betrayal, they would kill him. Wyatt later testified that he had also offered a reward to Frank McLaury for information about the identities of the cowboys, and Ike Clanton would later testify that Wyatt had admitted the Earps and Holliday were involved in the robbery themselves.

Clanton never got the chance to collect because the three cowboys that were responsible for the robbery and murder were killed in New Mexico after getting mixed up in a barroom brawl, but the secret between Earp and Clanton remained.

Ike Clanton

Harboring this secret did not ease Clanton's mind. He was convinced that Earp told Holliday about the arrangement, but Earp denied it. Clanton tried to goad Earp into admitting that he told Holliday by saying that Doc himself said he knew about the deal. Holliday was in Tucson when, on October 21, Wyatt sent Morgan to get him and ask him to return to Tombstone. Wyatt wanted to ask Holliday himself what, if anything, he knew. When Holliday arrived, he assured Wyatt he knew nothing about a deal between him and Ike Clanton, who had briefly left town to tend to other business.

Throughout the middle months of 1881, the resentment between the Earps and McLaurys also began to mount. When another stagecoach was robbed near Tombstone on September 8, it was determined that the robbers were Pete Spence and Frank Stilwell, both friends of the McLaury brothers. After they were arrested and released on bail, Virgil Earp arrested the pair again on October 13, either for a different charge or for a different robbery, but the McLaurys believed that Earp was harassing the two and arresting them for the same charge as before. Frank McLaury warned Morgan Earp that if the Earps arrested the McLaurys or their friends again, they were dead men.

Frank McLaury

On October 25, 1881, Clanton returned to Tombstone with Tom McLaury. The more he drank, the more his paranoia got the best of him. The more paranoid he got, the more he talked, and several people said they heard him make threats about killing Wyatt. When Holliday saw Clanton at the Alhambra Saloon, he directly confronted him and suggested that he stop saying that Earp had betrayed him. By now, Clanton was extremely drunk and continued his threats. Holliday responded by calling Clanton a liar. The incident was on the verge of escalating into a gunfight when Virgil intervened and threatened to arrest them both.

When Clanton saw Wyatt later in the evening, he told him he would get him in the morning. Wyatt ignored Clanton and went home to bed. Clanton, however, did not go to bed. He made his way to the Oriental for more drinking and a poker game with Behan, and, of all people, Virgil, who played cards that night with a pistol lying across his lap.

The Gunfight at the O.K. Corral

The O.K. Corral in 1882

When the Earps and Holliday woke up the next morning, October 26, 1882, they were told that Ike Clanton was walking the streets of Tombstone, going from saloon to saloon to announce his intentions to kill them. Some said Clanton went into the telegraph office to wire for help, and the town began to buzz with concern that a gang of angry cowboys was about to descend on Tombstone. Holliday could not help but hear the rumors and went to help. Earp told him, "This is none of your affair," to which Holliday said, "That is a hell of thing to say to me."[10] After the events that followed, many questioned why Holliday, known to have a quick temper, would be asked to help disarm the Clantons and the McLaurys, if that was Virgil Earp's intention.

In addition to Clanton's threats, Wyatt got into a physical confrontation with Tom McLaury, pistol-whipping him outside the courthouse after Tom had told him he was unarmed despite plainly and visibly carrying a revolver tucked near his right hip. It was for this reason that the Earps may have assumed Tom was armed when the gunfight started hours later.

No mob of angry cowboys ever appeared, but by the early afternoon, Ike Clanton had been joined by his brother Billy, cowboy Billy Claiborne, and Frank and Tom McLaury. The group of five were standing in a vacant lot on Fremont Street near the rear of the O.K. Corrall, in close proximity to where Holliday was renting a room and on the route to the homes of the Earps, possibly intending to serve a threatening warning to them. Around 2:30 p.m., Sheriff Behan attempted to persuade the cowboys to disarm themselves, but his request was quickly rejected.

---

[10] Roberts, 194.

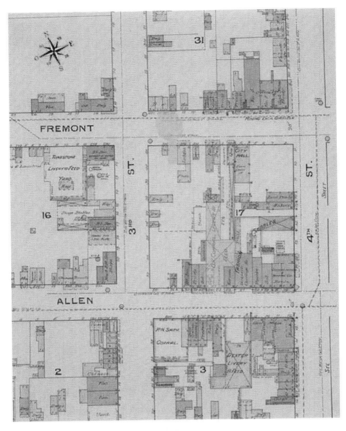

The O.K. Corral is in yellow. The fighting took place in the green circle and alley

At about 3:00 p.m., Wyatt, Morgan, and Virgil Earp, along with Holliday, headed to the lot to confront the cowboys. The Earps were carrying revolvers, while Holliday had a pistol and a shotgun given to him by Virgil, which he had concealed under his long coat to avoid alarming the citizens of Tombstone.

Despite the fact that the most famous gunfight in American history took place moments later, exactly how it all went down remains heavily disputed and not completely clear. The Earps claimed that Virgil approached the Clantons and the McLaurys, stopping within a few feet of them to inform them that they were under arrest. Some say that Billy Clanton and Frank

McLaury were about to surrender, while the Earps claimed that the two went for their guns. One resident, Martha J. King, claimed the Earps told Holliday to "let them have it" and initiated the gunfight.

Who started the shooting was disputed, but everyone agreed that two shots were fired almost simultaneously, touching off the firing. However it started, the gunfight lasted, by all accounts, about 30 seconds. When it was over, an unarmed Ike Clanton and Billy Claiborne had run away, but the McLaury brothers, including an unarmed Tom, were dead in the street. Billy Clanton had suffered a painful and fatal gunshot wound to the chest, still slumping near the corner of the Macdonald house, where he had been leaning when the shooting started. Virgil and Morgan Earp were wounded, as was Holliday. It is believed that Billy Clanton and Frank McLaury, even after being wounded, continued shooting, and one of them hit Morgan Earp across the back. Virgil thought Billy Clanton hit him in the calf and began firing at him after being injured. Frank McLaury hit Holliday in a pocket and grazed him, incensing him and leading him to chase after Frank shouting, "That son of a bitch has shot me, and I am going to kill him." Wyatt managed to walk away without so much as a scratch. According to Big Nose Kate, when Holliday came back to his room he openly wept, stating, "That was awful—awful."

Tom McLaury

In Tombstone, the initial reaction after the gunfight was that the Earps and Holliday were heroes. *The Tombstone Epitaph*'s described the shootout, "Wyatt Earp stood up and fired in rapid succession, as cool as a cucumber, and was not hit." The *San Francisco Examiner* suggested that Tombstone's residents be grateful to have the Earps on their side of the law.

However, that sentiment did not last long. Plenty of people in Tombstone believed that the three dead men were murdered in cold blood, and they wondered why the Earps would ever ask a hothead like Doc Holliday to help them disarm the McLaurys and the Clantons. The local undertaker displayed the three corpses in their coffins in his window with a sign that read, "Murdered in the Streets of Tombstone."

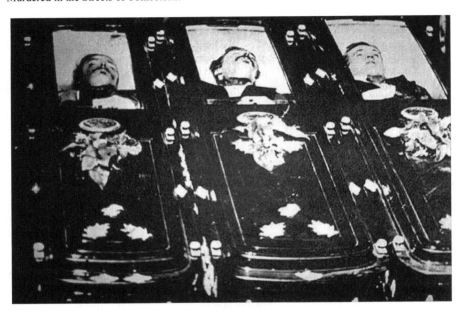

The corpses of Tom McLaury, Frank McLaury, and Billy Clanton were publicly displayed in the undertaker's window.

Ike Clanton filed murder charges against Holliday and the Earps. Wyatt and Doc spent 16 days in jail, while Virgil Earp was temporarily suspended as town marshal. Just over a month after the shootout, the case was brought before Justice Wells Spicer. Ultimately, he found in favor of the defendants, determining that there was too little evidence to indict the defendants and that the evidence that did exist suggested they had acted within the law. Still, the ruling further incensed many people in Tombstone and left Ike Clanton still wanting revenge. The tension and assassination threats directed at the Earps were enough to lead the federal government to take notice, particularly because the cowboys continued to run amok unchecked in Mexico and the government wanted to avoid an international incident.

The Earps Become Targets

It took little time for Clanton to get his revenge. On December 28, 1881, Virgil was ambushed in the street and shot in the arm by a shotgun blast as he left the Oriental Hotel. The shooter had hidden in drugstore that was under construction across the street. The force of the shot spun Virgil around and blew his arm into two, but he did not leave his feet until collapsing into Wyatt's arms back across the street. He would have no use of the arm for the rest of his life.

The shooter was never identified, but Ike Clanton's hat was found near where the shots had been fired. Clanton was later acquitted after several eyewitnesses testified he was not in Tombstone at the time of the shooting. In response to the attack on Virgil, Wyatt requested from the U.S. Marshal Crawley Dake that he be appointed a deputy U.S. marshal and given the ability to choose his own deputies, a request that was granted. The Earps racked up such expenses while bolstering their protection and swelling their ranks that Wyatt later had to mortgage his own house, and it was foreclosed on after he failed to repay the debt.

A few months after the attempt on Virgil's life, the Earp brothers' luck ran out. A few months later, in March 1882, Morgan Earp was playing pool in a billiards hall after attending a theater show. As he was playing, gunmen entered an alley outside the building and fired into the room, hitting Morgan in the spine. Wyatt was nearly hit by one of the bullets himself, which went straight over his head. As the gunmen escaped into the night, Morgan died within the hour.

Morgan Earp

The Earp Vendetta Ride

Now it was the Earps and Holliday's turn to seek revenge. Two days after Morgan's death, which happened to be Wyatt's 34th birthday, the grieving Wyatt made arrangements for Morgan's body to be sent to their father's home in Colma, California. Morgan was reportedly buried in a suit that belonged to Holliday. Virgil and his wife, Allie, left for San Francisco under the watchful eye of armed guards, and Holliday joined Wyatt when it was time for Virgil and Allie to board the train from Tucson to San Francisco.

As the train left the station in Tucson, Wyatt claimed to have seen Ike Clanton and Frank Stilwell lying in wait for Virgil. After a brief chase, Clanton got away, but Wyatt shot and killed Stilwell, leaving his body riddled with bullets by the railroad tracks. Though it was just days after the attack on Morgan, Wyatt may already have believed that Stilwell was one of the men who shot at Morgan. Pete Spence's wife later claimed that Spence and Stilwell were among a group of men who had returned home shortly after Morgan had been shot, and that Spence had threatened to harm her if she told authorities anything.

Stilwell

While Wyatt and his posse, which included Holliday and his brother Warren, continued its search for Morgan's killers, Sheriff Behan put together his own posse to search for Earp, now wanted for Stilwell's murder. Just before conducting his infamous month long "vendetta ride", Wyatt had a famous confrontation with Behan, who sought to meet with him, warning the sheriff, "Johnny, if you're not careful you'll see me once too often."

Warren Earp

Before Behan could find him, the vendetta posse killed a cowboy named Florentino Cruz, also known as Indian Charlie, based on a rumor that he was involved in killing Morgan. Soon thereafter, the posse killed Curley Bill Brocius, Wyatt's nemesis from a few years earlier, though there was no evidence that Bronchus was involved with Morgan's death. The lawless vendetta to avenge the killing of Morgan quickly erased any support he may have had from the residents or businesses of Tombstone.

By the time the Earp Vendetta Ride was over, the posse had killed four outlaws. On April 13, 1882, Earp and Sadie Marcus left Arizona and went to Gunnison, Colorado to weather the storm. Mattie had already left for California and was with Virgil and his family. Wyatt expected the same businessmen who had financed him on his "Vendetta Ride" to come through and work out a pardon for the crimes he had committed so he could return to Tombstone and run for sheriff. But by this time many in Tombstone were glad to have him gone, and after six months of waiting it was apparent that a pardon would never come. Earp and his new common-law wife, who would remain with him for the rest of his life, went west again and headed to San Francisco.

Wanted for murder and with little, if any, support from the town, it was time for Earp and Holliday to leave Arizona in Spring 1882. It was also time for the friends to part ways. Mattie Earp was already in California with Virgil, where she would wait in vain for Wyatt to return. He may not have become sheriff, but he did get Behan's woman, and Sadie Marcus would remain with Wyatt for the rest of his life. Earp and his new common-law wife headed to San Francisco, while Doc Holliday stayed in Colorado.

Chapter 6: Doc Holliday's Final Years

Holliday could not have returned to Arizona if he wanted to, at least not without facing a possible death sentence, but when he arrived in Denver in May 1882, he was arrested for Stilwell's murder. Behan made it clear that if Holliday appeared back in Tombstone, he would see to it that Holliday hanged and called for his extradition back to Arizona. With some intervention from Wyatt, who called on his old friend and the sheriff of Trinidad, Colorado, Bat Masterson, the extradition was blocked. Masterson had pulled some political strings, which evidently went as high as the governor's office.

The seminal moments associated with Holliday were now behind him, but Holliday's final years were marked by much of the same events as the prior 15 years of his life. He followed the gambling circuit around Colorado as his health permitted, never quite able to escape his reputation or bloodshed. Holliday and Wyatt were falsely accused of killing the cowboy Johnny Ringo, a friend of Ike Clanton's and Frank Stilwell's, in Arizona, though neither men were anywhere near the state at the time. It's possible that Doc was implicated simply because of the bad blood that previously existed between him and Ringo. In Tombstone in January 1882, only 3 months after the Shootout at the O.K. Corral, Holliday got into a heated argument with Ringo and allegedly said, "All I want of you is ten paces out in the street." A duel was stopped only by Tombstone's police, who arrested both of them.

Ringo

Though Doc almost certainly had nothing to do with Ringo's murder, Doc did indeed shoot Billy Allen in the arm over a $5 debt in 1884. This case actually went to trial, but on March 28, 1885, the jury believed that Doc had acted in self-defense, even if there was little evidence to support this.

The altitude of Colorado was not good for a man with consumption, and any gains he made in his battle against the disease in New Mexico and Arizona were soon wiped away in the Rocky Mountains. With his hair now gray, his body wasting away, and a growing dependence on alcohol to ease his misery, Holliday had a reunion with Earp in a hotel lobby in Denver in May 1885. Sadie watched the meeting from across the room, and both she and Wyatt were shocked at Holliday's appearance. When they parted, there were tears in Wyatt's eyes. Later in Denver, Holliday also ran into his old nemesis, Milt Joyce, but by the point in his life, Doc was not looking for trouble and left Joyce alone.

In May 1887, Holliday took a train to Glenwood Springs, Colorado. Glenwood Springs not only had gambling halls, it had waters that he hoped would help him the way the springs of New Mexico had. Unfortunately, they did not, and Doc's health deteriorated rapidly. In September, he developed pneumonia, from which he never recovered.

Naturally, Holliday's death has been the subject of controversy and speculation. On the morning of November 8, 1887, John Henry Holliday died at the Glenwood Hotel at the age of 36. Legend had it that as he lay dying, Holliday looked at his feet, presumably amused that he was dying with his boots off. For one of the West's most notorious gunslingers, Holliday and countless others probably assumed that he would "die with his boots on" in a gunfight. According to this legend, the nurses said that his last words were, "Damn, this is funny." Given his illness, however, modern historians believe Holliday would've been incapable of speaking coherently in his final days. It was also widely believed that Wyatt was there when Doc died, but Wyatt would not hear about his death for months. And even though Kate later claimed to have been there, most accounts say Holliday was alone when he died.

Given the course of Doc's life and death, perhaps it's not surprising that there is some speculation over his final resting place. It was believed that Doc was buried in Linwood Cemetery overlooking Glenwood Springs, but since it was November the frozen ground may have made it difficult for Holliday to actually be buried there, since it was was only accessible via a difficult mountain road. Holliday's biographer, Gary Roberts, has noted that other bodies were definitely transported to the Linwood Cemetery in November 1887, and that newspapers of the time stated Doc was buried there.

Even if Doc was buried there, the exact placement of his body was lost over time, leading the cemetery to erect a headstone in a random location on the grounds. However, the cemetery's initial headstone incorrectly listed the year of his birth as 1852 instead of 1851. Thus, it was eventually replaced by a more accurate headstone.

Chapter 7: Wyatt and Sadie Roam the West

Like Nick and Virginia Earp before them, Wyatt and Sadie Earp roamed across the West after leaving Colorado and after spending a brief stint of time back in Dodge City. Spending time in locations as diverse as San Diego, San Francisco, Alaska, Nevada, and Los Angeles, Wyatt was always on the lookout for the path to riches, but he could never completely escape controversy or the events in Tombstone.

San Diego

San Diego in 1885 was rampant with gambling fever. Its mild climate was an attraction then, as it is now, and it drew in businessmen, investors, and others who had newly acquired wealth. For a man who was as entrenched in the gambling world as Earp, San Diego offered a lot of opportunity. He and Virgil managed as many as four saloons and gambling halls, the most famous of which was the Oyster Bar in what was then referred to as the Stingaree District, but is now the historic Gaslamp Quarter. Located in a Victorian house on 5th Avenue, gambling was not the only attraction at the Oyster Bar. The Golden Poppy was a brothel located on the upper floor and featured brightly painted rooms with women in dresses to match.

San Diego also nurtured another passion of Earp's: horse racing. He won his first horse, Otto Rex, in a poker game and ran the horse on the California harness racing circuit in the late 1890s. Wyatt and Sadie left San Diego to follow the circuit in 1890 but returned occasionally over the next decade to tend to property they owned. Earp's success in the gambling halls allowed him to dabble in the San Diego real estate market, and he owned at least 10 properties between 1888 and 1890. When the time came to list his occupation for the 1890 San Diego City Directory, Earp listed his as "capitalist."

The legal and illegal business interests in San Diego led to a booming crime rate and, at one point, San Diego had one of the worst crime rates in the country. Robbery, assault, and murder were not out of the ordinary, but Earp was in San Diego to make money, not fight crime. Still, Earp was connected enough to wield influence over the local police department. He was friends with the mayor, William Hunsaker, and he had an understanding with City Marshal Joseph Coyne that if the local police went into saloons, they were to look the other way when they saw gambling.

While Earp prospered in San Diego, his previous common-law wife, Mattie, had fallen on hard times. Mattie had left for California with Virgil and his wife when Wyatt left Tombstone for Colorado. She waited there for word from Wyatt regarding where and when she should meet him. When word never came, Mattie returned to Tombstone, which by this time was beyond its prime years. Even resorting to her previous trade as a prostitute was difficult because there were not enough men in town with the money to pay. She was found dead from an apparent suicide following a lethal combination of alcohol and laudanum on July 3, 1888. When the local coroner launched an inquest into her death, a Pinal County laborer, T.J. Flannery, said, "Earp, she said, had wrecked her life by deserting her and she didn't want to live."[11]

Ike Clanton managed to evade Wyatt Earp's vengeance, but he was on the wrong side of the barrel on June 1, 1887. Detective Jonas Brighton pursued Clanton and his brother, Phineas, on charges of cattle rustling and caught up with them in Springerville, Arizona. Phineas surrendered, but when Ike resisted arrest, Brighton shot and killed him.

San Francisco

The Earps also spent several years in San Francisco. Always a sportsman, Earp still enjoyed boxing, an interest developed in his days of working the Union Pacific railroad camps. He fed his love for the sport by refereeing and judging boxing matches. Many times Earp traveled across the San Diego border into Tijuana to referee matches, where money could be wagered out of the sight of the American authorities. These matches were not for the faint of heart. In one match in June 1888, the crowd grew so raucous that the Mexican policemen who were called in

---

[11] Bell, Bob Boze. *The Illustrated Life and Times of Wyatt Earp.* Page 97.

responded by pointing their revolvers at the mob to regain control.

When asked to referee a boxing match in San Francisco on December 2, 1896, Earp agreed. This was no undercover brawl in a backroom of Tijuana. This was a heavyweight prizefight with a purse of $10,000 between the famed Ruby Bob Fitzsimmons and the up-and-coming Tom Sharkey. The British Fitzsimmons made history by becoming boxing's first champion in three different weight divisions. Believing that James "Gentleman Jim" Corbett had retired and relinquished his crown, this fight was billed as the heavyweight championship of the world. Fitzsimmons was heavily favored, although rumors persisted that the fight was fixed to favor Sharkey. Initially unable to agree on a referee, the fighters eventually agreed on Earp.

Fitzsimmons

Boxing at the close of the 19th century was dogged by claims that it was too brutal. It had been outlawed in many towns, but as more rules were put in place to protect the fighters and instill some civility, boxing was experiencing something of a revival. Therefore, many in the crowd at Mechanics Pavilion were surprised to see Earp climb into the ring with a revolver strapped to his hip. Perhaps it was a habit from his experiences in Tijuana, but nonetheless, Earp had to be asked to surrender his firearm before the match could begin, for which he was fined $50.

When the fight commenced, it went as expected for the first seven rounds. Fitzsimmons was in control and seemingly on his way to victory. In the 8th round, Fitzsimmons unleashed a powerful punch to Sharkey's lower abdomen, sending Sharkey to the canvas. Earp called the punch a low blow and awarded the match to Sharkey, setting off pandemonium as Sharkey had to be carried from the ring. Fitzsimmons and his manager, who had heard the fix rumors, were incensed, as were those in the crowd who had their money on Fitzsimmons. Fitzsimmons sued for the purse in court, but the judge found no evidence that Earp was part of any fix and, saying that holding the match in the San Francisco city limits was illegal, anyway, allowed Sharkey to keep the winnings.

Despite the ruling, Earp was subject to a relentless torrent of accusatory articles and cartoons from the *San Francisco Call*. Every day for a month after the fight, the newspaper printed something about Earp, claiming that the fight was fixed and he was involved somehow. Earp denied it all, saying he called the fight as he saw it, but it did nothing to calm the furor that was regularly fed by the local writers. Later, it was revealed that at least one of the sportswriters lost money on the fight and was making Earp pay by crucifying him in print. Nonetheless, Earp was still seen in the boxing community. He was present for another Fitzsimmons fight, this time in a bout against the now un-retired Corbett in Carson City, Nevada in March 1897. Earp was not asked to referee, but he was asked to be a bouncer.

Eventually, though, as was the case in Tombstone, Earp found himself an enemy in his own community. Finally fed up with the fallout from the fight, Earp sold all of his sporting assets and turned his attention north.

Alaska, Seattle, and Back Again

Earp in Alaska

Wyatt and Sadie followed the rush to Alaska, where gold had been discovered in the Klondike and near Nome. In 1899, Earp and Charles E. Hoxie opened the Dexter Saloon, although this was not Earp's only business venture that year. He also had business interests in Seattle, Washington.

Like it was in many towns that were opening in the West, gambling was rampant in Seattle. Technically, gambling was illegal there, but the level of tolerance fluctuated, and it was not hard to find in the city's Tenderloin District. John Considine was the leader of the Seattle gambling scene, and when Earp came into town in November 1899 with the intention of opening a gambling hall, Considine was not pleased. The people of Seattle were not sure what to think, either. Both the *Seattle Daily Times* and the *Seattle Post Intelligencer* made reference to Earp's debacle in the Fitzsimmons versus Sharkey match, although they could not agree on whether he was an evil troublemaker or an asset to the community.

After learning of Earp's business plans, a group of Considine's men paid Earp and his partner, local businessman Thomas Urquhart, a visit and suggested that they take their business outside of Seattle. If Earp could not agree to that, they told him to check in with the police chief, C.S. Reed, whom they assumed would not be happy to have Earp in town. Earp told Considine's crew in no uncertain terms that he was going to open his saloon and he was not going to line Reed's pocket with payoff money because he assumed Considine was paying him enough for the both of them.

Earp and Urquhart proceeded with their plans and opened the Union Club on Second Avenue. The politics of Seattle impacted whether or not gambling was legal or simply tolerated at any given time. When gambling was reinstated with a set of strict rules – which were broken enough that the city was collecting a windfall in fines – the Union Club was a good moneymaker for its owners. Urquhart was able to buy out Earp and he became the sole proprietor of the Union Club when Earp's brief stay in Seattle ended in 1900.

Alaska and Nevada

Nome, Alaska was yet another western boomtown when Wyatt and Sadie lived there in 1900. Parts of town were literally lined with tents, as gold prospectors were simply looking for a place to sleep before heading back out to look for gold. As was the case with other boomtowns, gambling, drinking, and prostitution were not hard to find. In an environment like this, it was also not difficult for Wyatt to end up in skirmishes with the law. On June 29, after he had been back in town for just about a month, Earp was arrested for interfering with an officer who was attempting to break up a street brawl. A few months later, Wyatt and Sadie's brother, Nathan, were arrested in the Dexter Saloon after being charged with beating an Army officer who tried to arrest a bar patron for disorderly conduct.

While Earp was in Alaska, his younger brother, Warren, was shot and killed in a barfight in Willcox, Arizona. The youngest of the Earp brothers, Warren worked as a bartender and a stagecoach driver. He was also notorious for being an angry drunk, frequently finding himself in trouble for his temper. Cochise County authorities declined to prosecute the shooter, ranch foreman Henry Hooker. Rumors that Earp left Alaska to seek vengeance for his brother's death were false.

Meanwhile, despite the fact that Earp had moved on, the San Francisco media continued to dredge up the controversy surrounding the Fitzsimmons/Sharkey match. In September 1900, a San Francisco sportswriter wrote a story about the history of the Earp family. The story was packed with lies, including the number of men Earp killed. Having grown tired of what he viewed as lies and misrepresentations of events, Earp began to think about writing his memoirs. His attempt to get his version of his life story in print would continue for the rest of his life.

On December 12, 1901, the *Los Angeles Times* reported the arrival of Wyatt and Sadie in Southern California after their stay in Alaska. While Wyatt claimed that his business interests in Nome were doing well financially, the fact that he never returned to Nome suggests otherwise. The Earps did find their way to Tonopah, Nevada, though. In 1902, Wyatt drove into town with a wagon full of bar fixtures and he opened the Northern Saloon. A friend managed the bar while Earp went off prospecting, but his stay in Nevada was not fruitful. After briefly holding a job as deputy to Marshal J.F. Emmit, Wyatt and Sadie made their way back to Los Angeles in 1903. They would spend their remaining years traveling back and forth between Southern California and Parker, Arizona, near the Colorado River. They had a mining claim there that never paid off, but Earp felt most at home when he was in the desert and, fittingly, he named the mine "Happy Days."

Wyatt's saloon in Tonopah, Nevada in 1902. It's very likely that his wife, Josie, is on the horse on the left.

South of Tonopah, in 1904, Virgil Earp worked as a bouncer for a saloon in the small town of Goldfield, which was thriving after the discovery of gold in 1902. In January 1905, Virgil was appointed deputy sheriff of Esmeralda County. Wyatt and Sadie joined Virgil and his wife there and put in some mining claims, but their stay was brief. Virgil contracted pneumonia and died on October 18, 1905. Soon after Virgil's death, his wife went to live near Virgil's family and Wyatt and Sadie returned to Los Angeles.

Los Angeles

Old frontiersmen started drifting into Los Angeles in the early 1900s. Many of the boomtowns were on their way to becoming ghost towns and a new industry - movies - offered opportunities for men used to real-life brawling to work as stuntmen. Some were even offered small roles on camera as extras. There was no need to worry about speaking lines; "talkies" did not begin until Al Jolson appeared in "The Jazz Singer" in 1927.

Wyatt Earp never appeared in a movie, but he did love watching them. Exactly how he earned a living during his years in Los Angeles is something of a mystery. It would not be unexpected for a former lawman and gambler to fall back on those skills whenever necessary. In October 1910, he was asked by the Los Angeles Police Department commissioner to ride out into San Bernardino County to remove those with illegal mining claims. A friend of the Earp family claimed that he served as Wyatt's deputy on special missions for the Los Angeles Police Department. Arthur King reported that he and Earp traveled into Mexico to track down fugitives of the law. Once located, King reported he and Earp brought the fugitives back to Los Angeles to stand trial, which was a quicker process than waiting up to two years for the Mexican government to extradite those who were wanted by the law.

Unfortunately for Wyatt, times were changing, and gambling was not as accepted as it had been in his heyday in Tombstone or even Nome. In July 1911, Earp was arrested for his role in an illegal game of faro, a favorite card game on the frontier, at a Los Angeles hotel. Wyatt was implicated as the organizer of the game, though he claimed he was merely a participant. Incensed at what he perceived as yet another assault on his character, he told his side of the story to the *Los Angeles Examiner*, and called on Henry Gage, the former governor of California, to serve as a character witness. The charges were eventually dropped due to a lack of evidence and this marked the last time that Wyatt, now in his 60s, would read his name in the paper as the result of skirmishes with the law.

Hollywood

The fact that movie sets were open during the silent movie era made it easy for the curious to wander around the movie lot and watch the filming. Earp was no exception. John Ford, who went on to become a legendary film director, once served Earp coffee on a movie set, and Earp counted Tom Mix, one of the first stars of Western films, as one of his friends. He also became acquainted with a young Marion Morrison and years later, after Morrison had taken the name John Wayne, he said he modeled his portrayal of western lawmen on Earp.

The Duke

When Earp was in Alaska, he also met author Jack London. The writer set two of his most famous novels, "White Fang" and "The Call of the Wild" in the Klondike Gold Rush. One day when London was in Los Angeles, he and Earp decided to track down former cowboy turned movie director, Raoul Walsh. They wanted to meet the man who had convinced Mexican revolutionary Pancho Villa to star in the 1914 biographic film, "The Life of General Villa."

As Walsh was taking a break at the movie studio, an assistant told him that two men were there to see him, one going by the name London. After confirming that the man named London had the first name Jack, Walsh told the assistant to send them in. The trio went to dinner at Al Levy's Café, owned by one of early Los Angeles' leading restaurateurs, Al Levy. The specialty of the house was a new sensation, oyster cocktails. While the men ate, one of the world's most famous entertainers, Charlie Chaplin, approached their table. When Walsh introduced his dinner guests to the movie star, Chaplin said to Earp, "You're the bloke from Arizona, aren't you? Tamed the baddies, huh?"[12]

Earp's best friend in Hollywood was William S. Hart, an actor, director, producer, and screenwriter. Hart portrayed men of the Western frontier before Tom Mix did, and their styles were very different. Hart's characters were dark and gritty, while Mix brought much more flair and flash to the screen. Earp told of his attempts to teach Hart the art of the "quick draw," but Hart dropped his gun so often during the transfer out of his holster that they had to put a towel on the floor to keep it from being damaged.

---

[12] Barra, Allen. "Wyatt on the Set!" *True West Magazine*, May 7, 2012.

The Quest to Set the Record Straight

As late as 1922, Earp was still the subject of scathing newspaper articles. *Los Angeles Times* reporter J.M. Scanland's story about Earp's days as a lawman, titled "Lurid Trails are Left by Olden Day Bandits," had at least one glaring error: it said that Earp was dead. Sadie was furious at the slanted article and contacted the *Times* to tell them so. Earp took it a step further two years later and went to the reporter's home to confront him, resulting in an effusive verbal and written apology.

Still, Earp wanted to more fully clear his name. John Flood and Earp met in 1905 and Flood, an engineer, became Earp's personal secretary. Flood made an attempt at writing the biography, but he was an engineer, not a writer. His manuscript was simply not well written. Sadie and Wyatt asked Hart to use his connections to help get the book published, but even a Hollywood heavyweight like Hart had no luck. Rejection letters came in with every attempt at publication, starting with a query to the *Saturday Evening Post* to see if the magazine was interested in serializing Earp's story. The feedback Earp and Hart received criticized both the content and the style of the manuscript. One publisher simply said that the story was not interesting.

Hart and Earp were discussing possibilities for suitable collaborators that might improve on Flood's manuscript when, in late 1928, Earp was approached by a writer from San Diego, Stuart Lake. Lake had served as press secretary during the presidency of Teddy Roosevelt, one of the nation's great outdoorsman and a lover of the West. Roosevelt had a conversation with Bat Masterson, one of the Wild West's most famous characters and a friend of Earp's. Masterson, among other things, was a former lawman, and, like Earp, an avid gambler and former deputy in Dodge City. Unlike Earp, though, Masterson left the West and started a career as a sportswriter in New York City around 1883. He never forgot about Earp, though, and told Roosevelt, with Lake listening, that it was Earp that really epitomized what the West was all about.

When Masterson died while typing his column for the *New York Telegraph* in 1921, Lake determined that if he was going to contact Earp and write his story, he needed to start trying to locate him before it was too late. When Earp finally heard from him, he liked Lake and his credentials. He told Hart in a letter that they had enjoyed his conversations with Lake and suggested that perhaps Lake would be the one to finally help him get his memoirs published. Even as Earp's health was declining, he was concerned with the accuracy of his life story in print.

The Earps lived far from the lap of luxury in Wyatt's final years. When not at their mining camp near Parker, they rented small, inexpensive bungalows close to downtown Los Angeles. Sadie's sister sent money regularly, but there were reports that she used that money to sustain her own gambling habit. Often, the Earps relied on the generosity of Charles Welsh and his family, friends from the Alaska days, who offered the Earps a place to stay.

On January 7, 1929, Earp wrote a letter to Hart and told him that his brother, Newton, had died at the age of 91 shortly before Christmas. Those close to the Earps knew that the end was near for Wyatt, too. Wyatt Earp died in his Los Angeles home on January 13, 1929 at the age of 80. It is reported that his last words were, "Suppose. Suppose."

Chapter 8: Wyatt Dies but a Star is Born

Wyatt Earp in later years, 1925

In a fitting tribute to the former lawman and true icon of the West, Tom Mix and William Hart, who portrayed lives on screen that Earp actually lived, served as pallbearers at Earp's funeral. Sadie was too distraught to attend. Earp's body was cremated and the remains were sent to Colma, California, where his gravesite attracts regular visitors.

While Wyatt Earp had developed a reputation – and not always a positive one – and many in the West knew of him, he was not actually famous when he died, let alone the household name that he is today. Even among those who knew who he was, it is not likely that anyone other than Sadie really knew Wyatt, other than tales about the 30 second gunfight in Tombstone, which itself had been largely forgotten decades earlier. Earp himself was partially responsible for this. It is accepted by a consensus of historians that both Sadie and Wyatt told versions of the truth, rather than the complete truth, about Earp's life.

After Earp's death, Stuart Lake moved forward with Earp's biography. Sadie fought to have the publication stopped, wanting to both protect Wyatt's reputation and avoid any mention of herself in the book. Lake assured her that he would protect Earp's legacy, and he kept his promise with a flattering, semi-fictional account of Earp's life in *Wyatt Earp: Frontier Marshal*. Published in 1931, his biography was not the first one to offer a sensationalized account of Earp's life. Walter Burns called Earp "The Lion of Tombstone" in his 1927 book, *Tombstone, An Iliad of the Southwest*, a publication that Earp feared would interfere with his attempts to get his own book in print. Years later, Lake, admitted to fabricating several of the quotes he attributed to Earp. However, it is important to keep the book in context. It was written during the Great Depression, and Americans were searching for escape and heroes more than harsh reality. Lake was also not a trained historian and did not set out to write a scholarly text.

Despite the inaccuracies, *Wyatt Earp: Frontier Marshal* set the wheels in motion for the birth of the legendary, even if inaccurate, Wyatt Earp. A glimpse of this was seen shortly before Earp died. The 1928 movie "In Old Arizona" was the first western talkie and featured Warner Baxter as Sergeant Mickey Dunn, charged with finding the robber of a Tombstone stagecoach. Raoul Welsh directed the film and the character of Dunn drew from Earp's life. It also marked the introduction of the singing cowboy, which became a popular movie attraction.

This was followed by numerous characters in books, movies, and television that were either loosely or closely based on Earp. As would be expected, the Gunfight at the O.K. Corral made great movie fodder, starting with 1932's "Law and Order." The film gave an account of the Gunfight at the O.K. Corral and was based on the novel "Saint Johnson," written by W.R. Burnett. The Earp character is named Frame Johnson and was first played by John Huston. In the remake in 1953, the future president, Ronald Reagan, portrayed Johnson. In 1934, Lake's book was made into the movie, "Frontier Marshal," this time with the name Michael Earp in place of Wyatt. The name Wyatt Earp was finally used in film in 1942 in 'Tombstone," featuring another retelling of the gunfight in Tombstone. Acting legend Henry Fonda played Wyatt in the 1953 film, "My Darling Clementine."

Earp made it to television in 1955, when westerns were all the rage. Hugh O'Brien played him in the ABC series, "The Life and Legend of Wyatt Earp," which aired until 1961. Joel McRae took his turn at playing Wyatt in the movie "Wichita" in 1955 and in 1957, one of the more acclaimed efforts involving Earp's legend, "Gunfight at the O.K. Corral" was released, starring Burt Lancaster as Wyatt. The film was nominated for two Academy Awards.

In 1971, Earp returned to the movies in "Hour of the Gun," starring James Garner. It was another 20 years before Earp would return to the silver screen, this time in the 1993 movie "Tombstone." Kurt Russell stars as Earp, and for the first time, his relationship with Sadie was explored in film with Dana Delaney playing Earp's third wife. A year later, Kevin Costner starred in "Wyatt Earp," which explored his life from his teen years through his prospecting days in Alaska.

Earp's image can be found in more than just movies. The U.S. Postal Service featured him on a postage stamp in 1994 as part of its Legends of the West Series. His name and likeness have been used to sell cap guns, clothing, pocket watches, and action figures. Fans of the West can easily find replica guns, hats, badges, and holsters. The small town of Tombstone continues to capitalize on Earp and the legendary gunfight that haunted him, offering a reenactment of the battle every afternoon.

Sadie Earp died in 1944. Glenn Boyer published what were originally believed to be her memoirs in "I Married Wyatt Earp" in 1976. However, after it was discovered that much of the book was fabricated, the University of Arizona Press removed it from its catalog, and historians no longer consider it a historically accurate document.

Long after his death, Wyatt Earp continues to be portrayed as a hero of the West, despite the fact that there it little evidence to suggest that he was one in any traditional interpretation of the word. He was a flawed man living in a time and place where society's rules and the nation's laws were not what they are today. The fact that Earp has been held up as symbol of the heroism of the West, over a century after he walked the streets of Tombstone, is largely the work of America's need for heroes, as well as the nation's desire to interpret its history through a glossier, more adventurous prism. Perhaps it is all the more fitting that Earp has become the most famous man of the Wild West, which itself continues to be widely celebrated for its lawlessness and viewed as uniquely American. .

Even if Earp was not a hero, there is no doubt that Earp was a survivor who lived a life that spanned an incredible series of events in America's history. A young boy during the Civil War and an elderly man just as the country was about to fall into the Great Depression, Earp saw an enormous amount of change in his country. Even for those who do not view Earp as a hero, he remains a symbol of the West and a link to the nation's past.

Chapter 9: The Doc Holliday Legend

Like other men of the Western frontier, especially his friend Wyatt Earp, Doc Holliday was as much myth as man after his death. At least part of his story has been depicted in film, including "My Darling Clementine" in 1936, "Gunfight at the OK Corral" in 1957, and "Tombstone" in 1993. Stacy Keach played him in the first movie to feature him as the main character in "Doc" in 1971. In 2011, Mary Doria Russell published the critically acclaimed novel, "Doc," a work of historical fiction that has been hailed by critics for shining new light on the man that everyone thought they already knew. Later that year, HBO announced that Doc would be getting his own television series, based on Russell's novel.

Doc Holliday did not lead the life that seemed to be his destiny. John Henry Holliday was an educated, handsome, and witty man could have been a dentist and a member of high society in the South. Instead, circumstances both within his control and outside of his control conspired to create Doc Holliday, who spent his adult life under the dark image of a cold-blooded killer in the West, a reputation that was unquestionably partly his own creation. In one interview with a newspaper, after being asked if his conscience ever troubled him, Holliday reportedly answered, "I coughed that up with my lungs years ago."

Holliday left behind no documents, no records, and no children to tell his story, leaving historians to piece together the life of a boy who grew up during the Reconstruction Era in the South and became an icon of the West. This has left much open to interpretation, making an accurate profile of his life extremely challenging. Virgil Earp himself may have summed it up best in an 1882 interview with the Arizona Daily Star, explaining, "There was something very peculiar about Doc. He was gentlemanly, a good dentist, a friendly man, and yet outside of us boys I don't think he had a friend in the Territory. Tales were told that he had murdered men in different parts of the country; that he had robbed and committed all manner of crimes, and yet when persons were asked how they knew it, they could only admit that it was hearsay, and that nothing of the kind could really be traced up to Doc's account."

Regardless of which Holliday stories are true or embellished legend, what is clear is that Holliday had no great achievements that might set him apart from other men of the 19th century. And yet he has become a household name, second perhaps only to Wyatt Earp among the legends of the West. Why is there so much interest in a man that many believe was a hotheaded gunman at best and a killer at worst, even if neither are completely accurate descriptions him? Perhaps it is in the empathy for the boy that lost his mother to the same dreaded disease that would kill him. Perhaps it is a measure of understanding for a man who could not have his one true love because she happened to be his cousin. Perhaps it is simply because the idea of a dentist running with the likes of Wyatt Earp is too good of a story to pass up. Whatever the reasons, Holliday the man will certainly continue to be obscured by Holliday the legend, which has made him an indelible figure of the West.

Wyatt Earp Bibliography

Barra, Allen. *Inventing Wyatt Earp: His Life and Many Legends.* New York: Carroll & Graf Publishers. 1998

Barra, Allen. "Wyatt on the Set!" *True West Magazine.* May 7, 2012.

Bell, Bob Boze. *The Illustrated Life and Times of Wyatt Earp.* Phoenix: Tri-Star Boze Publications, 1995.

Gatto, Steve. *The Real Wyatt Earp.* Silver City, New Mexico: High Lonesome Books, 2000.

Tefertiller, Casey. *Wyatt Earp: The Life Behind the Legend.* New York: Wiley and Sons, 1997.

Turner, Alfred, ed. *The O.K. Corral Inquest.* College Station, Texas: Creative Publishing Company, 1981.

Doc Holliday Bibliography

"Bat Masterson Not Impressed by Doc Holliday." *Territorial News.* December 15, 2010.

Bell, Bob Boze. *The Illustrated Life and Times of Doc Holliday.* Phoenix: Tri-Star Boze Publications, 1994.

Guinn, Jeff. *The Last Gunfight.* New York: Simon & Schuster. 2011.

Roberts, Gary L. *Doc Holliday: The Life and Legend.* Hoboken, New Jersey: Wiley & Sons. 2006.

Turner, Alfred, ed. *The O.K. Corral Inquest.* College Station, Texas: Creative Publishing Company, 1981.

Jesse James

Chapter 1: Early Years

The James family began its long association with Clay County, Missouri in 1842 when Robert Salle James moved there with his wife, Zerelda Cole James. Robert, a 24 year-old student at Georgetown College, a Baptist school in Kentucky, had gone to Clay County to visit his mother-in-law, but he and his new wife took a liking to the area, which reminded them of Kentucky. Robert left Zerelda in the care of his mother-in-law and returned to Kentucky to finish his education, earning a bachelor of arts on June 23, 1843. By all accounts, Robert was well regarded by his classmates.

Robert was also busy starting a family. Zerelda gave birth to Alexander Franklin James on January 10, 1843. Another son, Robert R. James, died shortly after his birth in 1845. And by the time Jesse Woodward James was born on September 5, 1847, Robert was the pastor at New Hope Baptist Church with a growing congregation approaching 100 people. In 1848, Robert earned a master of arts degree from Georgetown College and a year later, he helped found the Baptist college William Jewell in Liberty, Missouri. That was the same year that his daughter, Susan Lavinia, was born. Like many in Missouri, Robert James was also a farmer and a slave owner.

The James Farm in Kearney, where Jesse lived as a child

All of these facts make it surprising that Robert James decided to leave his family and his congregation to follow the gold rush to California in 1850. Theories vary; some say he went to escape the consistent nagging of headstrong Zerelda, while others say he went to preach and save the souls of the prospectors. His brother, Drury James, was there too, so it was also possible he went to visit him. Perhaps he simply wanted to get rich. Whatever the cause, three year old Jesse cried and begged his father not to go.

Robert's decision was fateful, and his stay out west proved short lived. On August 18, 1850, Robert came down with cholera and died in a gold camp near what is now Placerville, California. Zerelda remarried Benjamin Simms two years later, a man a bit older than her who had little affection for her children. By the time Benjamin died in 1854 after being thrown by a horse, he and Zerelda had already separated.

In 1854, Dr. Rueben Samuel moved to Greenville, Missouri, just three miles from Zerelda's farm. He opened a medical office in the store owned by William James, Robert's brother. A year later, on September 26, 1855, Rueben and Zerelda were married. Zerelda requested that Rueben sign a prenuptial agreement, leaving her the six slaves and 200 acres of land should the marriage not last. The marriage did last, and Rueben eventually gave up medicine to work the family tobacco farm.

Zerelda James

Not much is known about the details of Jesse's childhood. Frank was said to be one that liked to instigate trouble, then stand back and watch. Jesse was not much different from other boys growing up in rural Missouri, finding himself in a scuffle from time to time, but nothing out of the ordinary for the time or place. Both boys went through at least elementary school, and somewhere along the way Frank developed an affinity for the works of William Shakespeare.

Chapter 2: Bleeding Kansas and the Civil War

Even though Jesse hardly knew his father, he inherited Robert's views on slavery and abolition. Robert James wanted no part of Northerners encroaching on what he viewed as the South's God-given right to own slaves and conduct business as they saw fit. The mid-19th century was a time of divisiveness in the nation as the United States looked toward westward expansion while having to address the institution of slavery, which threatened to tear the country apart. Missouri was a center of that battle since its application for statehood in 1819, and even though Missouri was admitted to the Union as a slave state, the issue was an extremely volatile one.

As it turned out, Jesse James would grow up during one of the most precarious eras in American history, and ultimately it would help lead him down the path he chose. The issue of whether Missouri would be a free state or slave state had been decided over a generation earlier, but throughout the 1850s, American politicians tried to sort out the nation's intractable issues. In an attempt to organize the center of North America – Kansas and Nebraska – without offsetting the slave-free balance, Senator Stephen Douglas of Illinois proposed the Kansas-Nebraska Act.

The Kansas-Nebraska Act eliminated the Missouri Compromise line of 1820, which the Compromise of 1850 had maintained. The Missouri Compromise had stipulated that states north of the boundary line determined in that bill would be free, and that states south of it could have slavery. This was essential to maintaining the balance of slave and free states in the Union. The Kansas-Nebraska Act, however, ignored the line completely and proposed that all new territories be organized by popular sovereignty. Settlers could vote whether they wanted their state to be slave or free.

When popular sovereignty became the standard in Kansas and Nebraska, the primary result was that thousands of zealous pro-slavery and anti-slavery advocates both moved to Kansas to influence the vote, creating a dangerous (and ultimately deadly) mix. Numerous attacks took place between the two sides, and many pro-slavery Missourians organized attacks on Kansas towns just across the border. Living in Clay County, young Jesse grew up in a part of Missouri that was dubbed "Little Dixie" for its pro-Southern sentiments and Southern culture. Jesse was nine years old when the Kansas-Missouri Border War broke out, but for five years he witnessed the bloody violence that accompanied the border war. By the time the Civil War started in 1861, there was little doubt which side Jesse and his brother, Frank, would take.

Jesse was still too young to fight in the unofficial border war, but the best known abolitionist in Bleeding Kansas was a middle aged man named John Brown. A radical abolitionist, Brown organized a small band of like-minded followers and fought with the armed groups of pro-slavery men in Kansas for several months, including a notorious incident known as the Pottawatomie Massacre, in which Brown's supporters murdered five men. Over 50 people died before John Brown left the territory, which ultimately entered the Union as a free state in 1859.

When the Civil War finally broke out in 1861, the border states of Kentucky and Missouri became even more important. By remaining neutral and not seceding, they became battlegrounds between the Union and Confederate forces, and Kentucky was so important that President Lincoln himself famously said, "I hope to have God on my side but I must have Kentucky."

The unsettled nature of the politics also dictated the nature of the fighting there, which would be dominated by guerrillas and "bushwhackers". By 1862, the battle lines in the Western theater had shifted well south of Missouri, leaving it firmly in Union control. Frank James joined the Confederate army, but when the Union dominated the rebel forces in Missouri, Clay County became occupied territory. Meanwhile, the state had its own militia and took the position that anyone associated with the Confederacy was a traitor. Anyone believed to be a Confederate or assisting the Confederacy risked a raid from the militia.

Thus, Confederate sympathizers fought what could loosely be called a counterinsurgency, sparking savage guerilla warfare in the woods and fields of Missouri. Cattle were confiscated on behalf of the Union, houses were burned, and pro-slavery sympathizers were lynched on their own property. Union civilians were murdered in their own fields in retaliation.

By 1864, the violence within the state began to slow down, but a small, militant faction remained committed to aggression against the Union for humiliating the Confederates, as well as persuading others from supporting the federal government. Known as the bushwhackers, the guerilla soldiers of western Missouri operated outside of the chain-of-command of the Confederacy, seeking vengeance with no small dose of extreme violence.

Frank joined one of the dozens of bushwhacker groups, with Jesse, now 15 years old, sometimes serving as a messenger between his mother and the band of guerilas Frank rode with. When Union soldiers came to the Samuel-James farm to get more information on Frank's location, Rueben initially would not comply. However, when the Union men strung him up and hung him from a tree, with Zerelda standing nearby, unleashing a verbal barrage upon the Union militia, Rueben eventually gave in and led the men to the bushwhackers' hiding place. The militia interrupted a poker game and the guerilas scattered. Frank got away with some of the other men, leaving two dead bushwhackers behind. After the bushwhackers regrouped, they were attacked again and lost more men in the fight.

Though he ultimately relented and gave the Union militia the information they wanted, Rueben was taken to Liberty, Missouri and jailed for aiding the Confederacy. Soon after that, he was transferred to St. Joseph. He was paroled on June 24, 1863. Zerelda was paroled in St. Joseph on June 5 after she signed an oath pledging her loyalty to the Union, which she, of course, had no intention of honoring. A letter dated July 8, 1863 was found in Rueben's file with the provost marshal and was signed by three neighbors. It addressed the incident at the farm and his initial refusal to assist the Union men, which led to his arrest. The letter said:

"In the case of Dr. Reuben Samuel, held as prisoner by the military, to report at Saint Joseph, we his neighbors, desire to state that we regard him as a peaceable, quiet, and inoffensive man, who would harm no one. He is, we hesitate not to state, under the control of his wife [and] stepson, and is really afraid to act contrary to their wishes on anything. This fear, we believe, caused him to make a false statement, which he would not, otherwise, have done. We know no man who is more peacefully inclined and who is more inoffensive. We therefore request you to discharge him."[13]

Though Jesse wanted to join his brother with the bushwhackers, he was brushed off as being too young, not to mention the fact he had other responsibilities at home with his parents in jail and a tobacco farm to tend. It did not help his cause when he blew off the tip of a finger cleaning a gun, earning him the nickname "Dingus" from the guerillas.

It is believed that Jesse finally got his chance to join up with the bushwhackers in the spring of 1864. Lt. Charles "Fletch" Taylor was in Clay County on a recruiting trip and likely encountered Jesse at that time. As a bushwhacker, Jesse saw violence on a horrific level. Men were not simply murdered, but some were scalped or disemboweled. Other Union men had their noses and ears cut off, their skulls crushed, or their throats cut. Fighting occurred at close range with revolvers rather than rifles. Bushwhacker units often carried multiple guns with them, allowing them to fire off six shots from one gun, six from another, and sometimes, six more shots from a third revolver, all at close range. Jesse survived a gunshot that passed through his upper chest and out the other side of his body. He was taken to Kansas City and spent two months recuperating at the home of his uncle, John Mimms. His cousin, Zee, kept a close watch over him until he was ready to return to the fighting.

The man who served as Jesse's mentor was a cold-blooded psychopathic killer named William T. Anderson, also known as "Bloody Bill." Before the Civil War, Anderson was a horse thief, and when it began he was part of the pro-Union "Jayhawkers" before he switched sides and worked with William Clarke Quantrill, perhaps the most famous bushwhacker in the region and considered by many to be the most vicious killer of them all. It is believed that Frank James may have also been part of Quantrill's Raiders, which became notorious for the August 1863

---

[13] Ted P. Yeatman, *Frank and Jesse James: The Story Behind the Legend,* Page 41.

massacre of 200 men and boys in Lawrence, Kansas, an abolitionist center. Jesse's mother would later name her daughter Fanny Quantrill Samuel after the notorious killer.

Bloody Bill Anderson

Quantrill

In the summer of 1864, Jesse joined Anderson, who led his band of guerillas on a murderous rampage. Known to decorate the saddle of his horse with Union scalps, Anderson was not afraid to take risks and start a fight even if he was outnumbered. His campaign of violence peaked in Centralia, Missouri on September 27, 1864, when he led a group of guerilla soldiers into Centralia and pillaged the town, murdering 22 unarmed Union soldiers along the way. When over 100 Union soldiers pursued the rebels, Anderson and his men were waiting and successfully ambushed them, killing even those who attempted to surrender. Many of the soldiers were tortured, and some were beheaded. This bloody massacre was Jesse's introduction to a violent life that he would never leave behind. When Anderson was caught and killed near Albany, Missouri a month later, a rope that he used to track the number of murders he was responsible for had 54 knots.

After the Centralia massacre, Zerelda was very proud of her sons, never swaying from the belief that they were Confederate heroes. However, in January 1865, Rueben and Zerelda received official orders from the Headquarters of the Department of Missouri accusing Zerelda of being disloyal to the federal government. She and her family were ordered to go under the supervision of an armed guard to either Memphis or Little Rock, whichever location they chose. However, they opted to hide out in Rulo, Nebraska, where Zerelda may have taught school and Rueben might have tried to revive his medical practice. They did not return to Missouri until the Civil War was over.

As the war finally drew to a close in April 1865, the bushwhackers initially did not believe it and thought it was just another Yankee lie. However, even after it was verified, Jesse James and the bushwhackers did not quit fighting on behalf of the Confederacy. After heading to Texas with Anderson's bushwhackers near the end of the war, Jesse returned to Missouri in time for a Wisconsin cavalryman to shoot him during a skirmish in May 1865, sending a bullet through his lung. Jesse was sent back to Kansas City to recuperate once again and made his way to Rulo, no doubt under the care of his stepfather. He was also tended to by first cousin Zerelda Mimms, who was named after Jesse's mother, and nearly a decade later Jesse would make her his wife. During his recuperation, according to his mother, Jesse said that he did not want to die but, if he did, he did not want to be buried in a northern state. She vowed that would not happen.

In May 1865, Missouri crafted a new, voter-approved state constitution. The state's slaves were freed and in order to vote, men had to take an oath verifying that they had not committed disloyal acts against the United States. This resulted in sweeping changes in local politics, including in Jesse James's home county, as any last vestiges of the Confederacy were removed. That August, Zerelda and her husband returned home, and soon after that Jesse and Frank joined her. As Missouri politics shifted toward an acceptance of Union values, particularly regarding emancipation, Jesse and other guerilla fighters resisted. While some former Confederates were able to move forward, Jesse either could or would not. He, like many of the other bushwhackers, viewed himself as a victim and believed he was being persecuted because of his role in the Civil War. Thus, the resistance of the bushwhackers would continue, albeit in another form.

Chapter 3: A Bushwhacker Becomes a Bank Robber

The war may have been officially over, but it was not over as far as the guerilla armies were concerned. Bushwhackers were believed to have been responsible for the theft of $58,000 from the Clay County Savings Association in February 1866, and after Jesse became famous he was tied to that robbery, but there is no evidence to support that Frank or Jesse had anything to do with it. Nevertheless, the fact the bank was owned and operated by Republicans who had been part of the Union militia made it a clear target for bushwhackers.

The Clay County Savings Bank

There were a string of bold armed robberies in broad daylight conducted by bushwhackers that Jesse was associated with, particularly Archie Clement's men. In later years, eyewitnesses to some of these robberies would claim that the James brothers participated, and after an 1867 robbery one man claimed "positively and emphatically that he recognized Jesse and Frank James ... among the robbers." Still, there was no clear connection made between a bank robbery and Jesse James until December 7, 1869. Jesse was on the lookout for Samuel P. Cox, the member of the Union militia that killed Bill Anderson. Jesse and another man – most likely Frank - went to Gallatin, Missouri and robbed the Daviess County Savings Association after asking for small bills in exchange for a 100 dollar bill. During the robbery, respected community citizen and family man Captain John W. Sheets was fatally shot in the heart and head. Sheets was working as the bank's cashier, and Jesse mistakenly believed that Sheets was Cox, so he murdered Sheets on the spot while getting away with less than $1,000.

Although the James brothers managed to escape and get out of town, Jesse bragged about avenging Bloody Bill's death to anyone who would listen, despite the fact he was wrong. Naturally, that had the effect of implicating him in the robbery and murder, and Gallatin was in an uproar. The governor of Missouri offered a reward for the capture of Jesse and Frank, and the *St. Joseph Gazette* provided details of the robbery and murder. Mentioning Jesse and Frank by name as the suspects, the article marked the first time that Jesse's name appeared in print in connection to a crime. It was exactly what Jesse had been waiting for. For a man who spent much of his brief life seeking attention, he had it now, and with the help of a newspaperman from Kansas City, Jesse James would soon become a household name.

John Newman Edwards was a former officer in the Confederate army who worked as an editor at the *Kansas City Times*. An alcoholic who was still bitter over the war, he was eager to stir up the former Confederates within the Democratic Party. His interests were purely political, as he wanted the ex-Confederates to resume their place of power. He saw the story in the *Gazette* about Jesse and Frank James and, with it, an opportunity to spread propaganda about the former Confederates of the Civil War, which in turn could potentially help his cause. He had already shown no hesitancy to portray armed rebels as victims of radicals from the North.

Edwards

Edwards met with Frank and Jesse and quickly realized that Jesse sought the limelight far more than Frank did. Jesse possessed almost an urgency to be noticed and this played well into Edwards' desire to create a story about the unfair treatment of ex-Confederates. About six months after the robbery in Gallatin, Jesse wrote an open letter to the governor, which Edwards printed in the *Times*. Jesse claimed that he was innocent of the charges against him and that the Union men were the true criminals. Jesse said that he was being unfairly cast as an outlaw simply because he held beliefs that were different from the Union. The creation of the mythical Jesse James was underway.

It was Edwards who started the myth that Jesse was the modern day Robin Hood who stole from the rich to give to the poor. In 1873, he devoted 20 pages to the James gang, glorifying their achievements as noble and for the greater good. Jesse was so enamored with the image that Edwards would create for him that he named his son, Jesse Edward James, after Edwards, although Jesse, Jr. was known as Tim. To make sure there was no doubt that he had been there, Jesse even took to leaving press releases at his crime scenes. He had no difficulty trying to live up to the image Edwards created, usually dressing in style and carrying a Bible that looked like it had been referred to often.

Chapter 4: The James–Younger Gang

The Younger Brothers and their posse

The James brothers had certainly committed their first notorious robbery before the end of the decade, but they were just getting warmed up. Even while Jesse was asserting his innocence in papers, the James brothers were forming a gang of robbers by linking up with the Younger brothers, Cole, John, Jim and Bob. The James-Younger Gang would also include Clell Miller and other former Confederate guerrillas and sympathizers. As the most notorious and the one with a public persona, Jesse became the face of the group, and though he was often assumed to be its leader, it appears the group shared power and decision-making.

Cole Younger

Cole, Jim, John, and Bob Younger formed the core of the James-Younger gang along with Jesse and Frank. Other men came and went from the group, participating in various armed robberies that occurred over Jesse's 15-year run as an outlaw. The James and Younger brothers moved freely about their home turf in Missouri. Thanks to Edwards, the public was convinced that the gang was on a noble pursuit. They not only did not turn the gang in, they helped shield them from the law, making the task of finding Jesse and his gang very difficult for Missouri authorities. This coincided with ex-Confederates winning back their seats in the state Senate. The conditions were ripe for the mythical Jesse to flourish.

It is no coincidence that Jesse's wife had the same first name – Zerelda – as his mother. Zee, as she was more commonly known, was named after Jesse's mother. Zee's mother was Robert James's sister, making Jesse and Zee James first cousins. The two met in 1865 when Jesse was recuperating from his gunshot wounds in Kansas City. Jesse and Zee had a long engagement, but after nine years, during which time most of Jesse's energy was spent on the exploits of the James-Younger Gang, the two were married at a family home on April 24, 1874 in Kearney, Missouri. By all accounts a plain woman, Edwards portrayed her in the press as a God-fearing Christian of striking beauty. While that characterization may not have been accurate, there is no doubt that she was loyal to her infamous husband. A year after they were married, Zee gave birth the Jesse, Jr. She had twins on February 28, 1878, but they both died. A year after that, on June 17, 1879, Zee and Jesse welcomed daughter Mary Susan James to the world.

In June 1871, Jesse and his gang arrived in Croydon, Iowa as many of the town citizens were at a local Methodist church to hear Henry Clay Dean give a speech. Dean was known throughout the region as an entertaining speaker, and he was also an outspoken critic of President Abraham Lincoln. While many in the town were distracted by Dean, the James–Younger Gang stole $6,000 from the Croydon State Bank. Rather than simply taking the money and running, the gang, not wanting to be upstaged by Dean, went to the church and brashly displayed the money they had stolen.

That crime brought additional attention to Jesse James, and it was an indication that James and his gang were operating across multiple states. In fact, the gang would operate as far south as Texas and as far east as West Virginia. Powerless to stop outlaws like James, banks began turning to the Pinkerton Detective Agency in an attempt to track them down. In the 1850s, Allan Pinkerton had established a private detective and security guard agency in Chicago, a forerunner of sorts for both private investigators and the Secret Service. A decade later, the Pinkertons, as the agency was informally called, claimed to have uncovered and thwarted a plan to assassinate President Abraham Lincoln, and from there they created the first secret service in the U.S. during the Civil War. In an effort to fight back against the notorious outlaws that targeted the nation's railroad system, railroad companies such as Union Pacific hired the Pinkertons to join forces with their own police force to capture the outlaws that preyed on their trains. Now the banks were getting in on the act and hiring the Pinkertons to protect them as well.

Allan Pinkerton

Allan Pinkerton's son Robert was sent to Missouri to find Jesse and Frank, and with the assistance of a local sheriff, Robert Pinkerton tracked the gang to a farm in rural Missouri. However, the gang got away and a few weeks later, Jesse sent another letter to the local press, again claiming that he was an innocent victim.

The following year, Jesse's gang rolled into Columbia, Kentucky, intent on robbing a bank. When the cashier, R.A.C. Martin refused to open the safe, one of the bandits turned to leave, then turned back around and shot the man in cold blood. Later that year, Jesse and two of the Younger brothers went to the Second Annual Kansas City Industrial Exposition. In front of thousands of witnesses, they robbed a ticket booth and got away with about $900, but a little girl was shot in the fight with the ticket seller. Jesse again wrote a letter to the paper, denying any involvement by him or the Youngers in harming the child. However, Cole Younger was furious that his name was being mentioned in print in any capacity with the crime. Edwards seized the opportunity to write an editorial titled "The Chivalry of Crime" and compared the bandits to President Ulysses S. Grant, the former Union general. Edwards said that Grant had stolen millions of dollars from Americans, whereas Jesse and his gang stole from the rich to give to the poor.

Over the next several months, the James-Younger gang robbed banks, trains, and stagecoaches in Missouri, Iowa, Louisiana, and Arkansas. In 1874, the Adams Express Company gave the Pinkertons another shot at finding Jesse. Missouri Governor Silas Woodson had already put up a $2,000 reward and secured funding from the state legislature for a private police unit to look for him, but he had no luck. There were too many places for Jesse and his gang to hideout, and too many people willing to help them

Adams Express crossed paths with the James-Younger Gang in the afternoon of January 31, 1874 when the Little Rock Express approached the tiny town of Gads Hill, about 100 miles south of St. Louis. Were it not for the railroad, it is not likely that Gads Hill would have merited any attention at all considering it was home to a grand total of 15 residents. Most of those residents met Jesse and his gang when they were herded near the train platform at gunpoint and robbed. Some say they were locked in a house, while others say they were kept near the platform, but either way the James-Younger Gang kept a close watch over them until the train arrived at 5:15.

The train's conductor, C.A. Alford, brought the train to a halt when he saw the red "danger" flag signal him. The bandits jumped onboard the train, telling Alford to keep quiet if he didn't want to get his head blown off. After robbing the baggage car, they moved on to the safe in the Adams Express car, which netted them over $1,000. Before moving on, they took the conductor's revolver and tobacco. From there, it was on to the passenger car. Alford recalled, "They weren't careful with the passengers. They punched them in the ribs with pistols and pointed their shooting irons into their faces. Not a man escaped. Everyone was robbed…"[14]

Those robbed included a sleeping car porter, who forked over his two dollars, and a "train boy" was relieved of $40. As the bandits made their way through the train, Frank quoted Shakespeare, one of the men wrote "robbed at Gads Hill" in a receipt book, and another outlaw exchanged hats with one of the passengers. When all was said and done, the first train robbery in Missouri in peacetime earned the James-Younger gang over $6,000. As he left the train 40 minutes later, Jesse left a press release with a passenger, with the request that it be sent to the *St. Louis Dispatch*. It read:

> "The most daring train robbery on record. The southbound train on the Iron Mountain Railroad was robbed here this evening by five heavily armed men and robbed of …
> dollars. The robbers arrived at the station a few minutes before the arrival of the train, and arrested the Agent, put him under guard, and then threw the train on the switch.
> The robbers are all large men, none of them under six feet tall. They were all masked, and started in a southerly direction after they had robbed the train, all mounted on fine-blooded horses. There is a hell of excitement in this part of the country."[15]

Acting on behalf of Adams Express, the Pinkerton agency sent undercover agent John W. Whicher, to track down Jesse in March 1874. When Whicher got to Clay County and asked where Jesse lived, the sheriff advised him not to go out there. He told Whicher if one of the James boys didn't kill him, their mother would. The next day, Whicher's body was found with

---

[14] Yeatman, Page 21.
[15] Yeatman, Page 22.

six bullet holes and a note pinned to him saying that this is what would happen to agents who went looking for the James brothers.

After Whicher's death, Allan Pinkerton took it so personall that he now made it his personal mission to take down the James-Younger Gang. The lawlessness was also becoming a political issue for local Democrats, who were criticized for their inability to stop Jesse and Frank. On January 25, 1875, the Pinkertons took another run at the James boys when three of the agents, with backup from Clay County locals, surrounded Zerelda's house. Shortly after midnight, Pinkerton ordered that the James farmhouse be firebombed. At this point, he was embarrassed and desperate, willing to try anything.

The Pinkertons first tried to set the house on fire by shooting a kerosene-soaked object at it. Rueben put out the initial fire by removing the burning siding. The Pinkertons then tried some type of firebomb, made of a hollow iron ball filled with combustible jelly. One of the agents broke a window and tossed the bomb into the house, setting a quilt on fire. Zerelda was able to throw the quilt out the window while Rueben got a shovel and threw the bomb toward the fireplace, where it exploded. Jesse's half-brother, Archie, was hit and killed by the flying shrapnel. A servant was also hit and seriously wounded, as was Zerelda, who had to have her right arm amputated below the elbow. All the while, Frank and Jesse were nowhere to be found.

To say that the Pinkerton attack was a disaster would be an understatement, and after that episode public sentiment was now squarely in the bandits' favor. Some in Missouri's state government even went so far as to propose a bill offering the James-Younger gang amnesty, a measure that was barely defeated, and many people came to believe that Jesse was telling the truth and truly was a victim of a manhunt by vicious radicals.

Most also correctly suspected that this obviously illegal act by the Pinkertons would not go unanswered. The underground intelligence system that aided the James brothers told them that Jack Ladd was the Pinkerton detective who threw the grenade and that he had infiltrated the area by working on Daniel Askew's farm. Jesse and Frank pursued Ladd for over a week before discovering that he had left the state, but Askew was easier to find, given that he lived a short distance from their mother's farm. Jesse rode out to Askew's house on April 12, 1875, not knowing for sure what Askew did but not caring for an explanation. Upon confronting Askew, James shot him to death in his yard. Allen Pinkerton's dream of catching Jesse James was finished.

Chapter 5: Northfield and the End of the James–Younger Gang

In the summer of 1875, Frank James was ready to give up his life of crime. He had just married Annie Ralston, a local schoolteacher, before the Pinkerton raid, and she urged him to give up being an outlaw. Frank's personality was the opposite of Jesse's. Whereas Jesse was hot-tempered and sought the limelight, Frank was more shy and unassuming. And even though the Pinkerton raid did not catch Frank and Jesse, it had persuaded them to get out of town and go into hiding for a while. They moved to the Nashville, Tennessee area and lived under assumed names. When Edwards began to talk about getting amnesty for Frank and Jesse for their war crimes, Frank was interested, but Jesse and Zerelda talked him out of it. Jesse was convinced that it was a ploy to get them to back into Missouri and that they would be executed if they went.

That summer, Jesse wrote a letter to the Nashville newspaper, again proclaiming his innocence. All the while, it is likely that he continued to rob banks in the South. Unlike his brother, he never entertained any intention of living a straight life, perhaps a result of the fact that he came to believe his press clippings and viewed himself as a Confederate war hero. With the South struggling through post-war Reconstruction, Jesse viewed the South in 1876 as the perfect environment to elevate his status, not pull back from it.

Ironically, the most famous robbery conducted by the James-Younger Gang was one in which Jesse's role is still the subject of debate. Sometime in the summer of 1876, Bill Chadwell suggested to his fellow outlaws in the James-Younger Gang that they rob a bank in his home state of Minnesota. He said he knew the area well and could ensure that they navigated their way in and out of the state safely. Despite the misgivings of Cole Younger and Frank James, the plan was hatched in the final weeks of the summer. Funding for the trip came courtesy of a train robbery in Otterville, Missouri on July 7. One of the gang members, Hobbs Kerry, had been caught and arrested in the aftermath of that robbery, but by the time he told the authorities who else was in on the robbery the James-Younger Gang was long gone. They had gone to Minnesota and traveled in small groups, each group doing their best to play the part of curious yet respectable businessmen, all the while scouting out the best location to pull off the robbery.

Ultimately, the gang decided to rob the First National Bank in Northfield. Some of the Younger brothers would later claim they picked the First National Bank because it had ties to Republican Adelbert Ames (who had governed Mississippi during Reconstruction) and his father-in-law, former Union general Benjamin "Beast" Butler. Butler was one of the most hated men in the South due to his time as military commander of New Orleans during the war. His rule over the occupied city was so controversial that Confederate President Jefferson Davis, a former friendly acquaintance of Butler's, ordered him to be summarily executed if ever captured. As it turned out, Ames held stock in the bank and Butler had no connection to it whatsoever.

Ames

When they arrived in Northfield on September 7, the eight outlaws broke into three groups. One group was to go inside the bank, one was to wait outside and be the lookout, and the other was to cover the getaway. It is believed that Jesse and Bob Younger, the two gang members who were most enthusiastic about the plan, went inside the bank with Frank. After they robbed the bank, all of the men planned to meet on the bridge that led to the Northfield town square. From there they would cut the telegraph wires and Bill would lead the way out of town. All agreed that no citizens were to be killed.

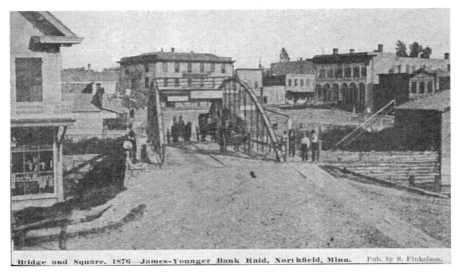

Bridge and Square, 1876 James-Younger Bank Raid, Northfield, Minn. Pub. by S. Finkelson.

At 2:00 p.m., Jesse, Frank, and Bob walked into the bank but did not completely close the door behind them, while Cole Younger and Clell Miller were outside the bank standing guard. Inside the bank, the gang encountered three men, Joseph Lee Heywood, Alonzo E. Bunker, and Frank J. Wilcox, who all denied being the cashier when told that their bank was being robbed. Jesse told Heywood that he knew he was the cashier and demanded that he open the safe, but Heywood refused. As Frank went to the vault to inspect the safe, Heywood ran toward Frank and shoved him, trying to trap him inside. Frank got away, but not before getting his hand and arm caught in the door. Bob Younger then pushed Heywood to the floor.

The main street and First National Bank

Out on the street, two men grew suspicious of Cole and Clell. J.S. Allen, owner of a hardware and gun store in town, walked toward the bank, but Clell grabbed him to stop him from going inside. Allen could see through the window that the bank was being robbed, and even though Clell told him to keep quiet as he shoved him away from the bank, Allen yelled out that the bank was being robbed and told anyone within earshot to grab a gun. Henry Wheeler, a medical student home from college on a break, joined in and began shouting a warning that their bank was being robbed. Clell shot at Wheeler and just missed shooting him in the head.

Before long, bullets were flying all over the street. Allen ran to his store and passed out guns to everyone in the vicinity of the shop. As Northfield's citizens armed themselves, the trio of bandits waiting on the bridge rode into town to join in the chaos. Inside the bank, Jesse wounded Heywood by slashing at his throat with his pocketknife when Heywood told him that he could not open the safe. Heywood said that there was a time lock on the safe, conveniently failing to mention that it had not been set. While Bob grabbed whatever loose money he could find and stuffed it in a sack, Alonzo Bunker chose that moment to try and get away. Bob shot him through the shoulder, but Bunker managed to keep his feet and ran out to the street through the back door as Cole came in the front door to report that they had to go.

Back outside, a citizen shot Clell Miller with light birdshot, the ammunition that the shop owner had put in a rifle in all of the confusion. The birdshot ripped at Clell's face and punctured one of his eyes, but he managed to stay on his horse and ride on through town. Anselm Manning, a citizen with a rifle, shot Cole in the shoulder, but Cole stayed on his horse and rode away without looking back. Manning also took out one of the gang's horses, shot Bill Chadwell dead with one shot to the heart, and finished off Clell with a shot that severed an artery in his shoulder. Wheeler, the medical student, had found a rifle and took a position in an upper story window, shot Jim Younger in the shoulder. In the bank, as Jesse, Frank, and Bob prepared to make their getaway, Frank shot Heywood in the head, killing him.

As Frank entered the street and climbed on his horse, he was unwittingly walking right into a shooting gallery and was almost immediately shot in the right leg. Jim Younger was shot again in the right shoulder and Bob took cover under a staircase. As Bob tried to shoot from his vantage point, he was shot in the elbow, a wound that would cripple him for the rest of his life. Charlie Pitts was also shot in the leg. Jim took another shot in his leg as Cole circled back to get to Bob. Cole was shot three times, but still managed to grab Bob and the brothers took off after Jesse, Frank, and Jim. As the remnants of the James-Younger Gang bolted out of town, with $26.76 in the bag of loot, the citizens of Northfield threw stones and pitchforks.

Much has been made of the incident at Northfield, Minnesota that resulted in the demise of the James-Younger Gang. For 15 years, they had terrorized parts of the West and the South, so it was unbelievable to some that a group of Minnesotans would be able to do what the law and the Pinkertons had not. Some speculate that the bandits must have been drunk. Others say that they lost the element of surprise and were too visible, creating suspicion. Perhaps it was simply because they underestimated their opponents. These were Civil War veterans and some had fought the Sioux in 1862. Most were deer hunters and knew how to use a gun. Whatever the reason, they did not back down when the former Confederates came into their town to try and take their hard-earned money.

The robbery attempt at Northfield was a complete disaster for the James-Younger gang, but agreement over what actually happened ends there. In fact, many historians now believe that Jesse James was not actually present at all, pointing to a lack of proof or evidence that he was present. Circumstantial evidence has bolstered this belief, including the fact he was never indicted for the crime and the belief that some of the gang attempted the robbery after drinking, something Jesse personally abstained from and would not have allowed before a job.

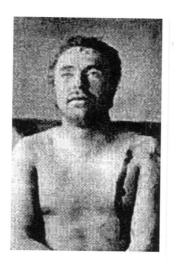

Photograph of Clell Miller's body

With Bill Chadwell dead in Northfield and without the sympathizing public willing to hide them from the law, the James-Younger Gang was in dire straits as it rode toward unknown territory in Minnesota. Everyone except Jesse (if he was there) was nursing wounds, but there was no time to stop. The telegraph wires had not been cut, as they had planned, and the citizens of Northfield alerted the neighboring towns of the bandits on the run. They were finally able to tend to their wounds near Dundas, Minnesota and stole a horse at gunpoint to even out the number of horses per man.

For two weeks, much of it in the driving rain, the gang searched for an escape route as posses pursued them through the Minnesota woods. More than once they came across a posse, but they pretended that they were also looking for the James-Younger gangs as well. What is known is that the James brothers eventually split off from the rest of the group and headed back toward Tennessee, perhaps because the wounded gang members were slowing them down. Whether or not the decision was unanimous is uncertain.

The end of the James-Younger Gang came in a swamp named Hanska Slough near Madelia, Minnesota. A group of men led by Civil War veteran James Glispin, now the local sheriff, tracked them there. Gunfire was exchanged and when it was over, outlaw Charlie Pitts was dead and the Younger brothers sustained more wounds, leaving them with little choice but to surrender. The Youngers were arrested and pled guilty to spare their lives, but Frank and Jesse were still on the loose.

Chapter 6: Final Years

After the fiasco in Northfield, Frank and Jesse stayed quiet for nearly three years. Northfield was the last straw for Frank, and he was ready to settle in on his farm near Nashville using the alias B.J. Woods. Jesse told everyone he was J.D. Howard, and the two were known by their neighbors only as law-abiding citizens. But as content as Frank was living a quiet life with his family, Jesse was restless. He tried to make money racing horses and playing cards, but he was not successful at either, and his money eventually started to run out. It also began to gnaw at him that he was no longer in the public eye; even his own children had no idea who Jesse James was. At a certain point, Jesse's nature got the best of him, and he became determined to return to life as an outlaw.

In the summer of 1879, Jesse headed back to Missouri to try and form a new gang, but it was nothing like his previous gang, and his recruits had neither the experience nor the loyalty that he had grown accustomed to over the past decade. Nevertheless, James and the new gang went on a crime spree throughout Missouri and the South, robbing a train in what is now Independence, Missouri and the paymaster at a canal project in Killen, Alabama. During another train robbery in Missouri, they killed a passenger and the train's conductor.

At the Independence crime scene, after they beat the express car manager with a gun, the gang left a press release trying to drum up more attention. This time, however, the public was far less interested in glorifying Jesse James, and John Newman Edwards no longer had any use for him. He had used him to support his cause of getting ex-Confederates back in political power. By 1880, with the Reconstruction Era over, Edwards had achieved his goal. When Jesse wrote to Edwards, who was by this time a severe alcoholic, Jesse received no reply.

In 1881, Jesse moved his family back to Missouri, settling in a small house in St. Joseph. He and Frank felt like the law was getting too close for comfort and it was time to leave Tennessee, but Frank did not join Jesse. He went on to Virginia. Now Jesse was without his brother, as well as the sympathy from citizens in his home state that had helped him elude the law the first time around. Many considered him to be a nuisance at best, dangerous at worst, and the new Missouri governor, Democrat Thomas T. Crittenden, persuaded railroad executives to pitch in on a $10,000 reward for Jesse and Frank. That money would prove to be tempting for someone who knew the famous outlaw.

By early 1882, Jesse was trying to put together yet another new gang, but he was running out of options. Now just a loose band of common thieves, Jesse was not even sure that he could trust the men in his gang. He grew increasingly paranoid and even murdered one of the members of his gang, Ed Miller. Convinced that Jim Cummins was out to get him, too, Jesse was in the process of hunting him down. The only two men that he thought he could really trust were Bob and Charley Ford. What Jesse did not know when he offered the Fords the chance to take part in robbing the Platte City Bank is that they had already agreed to a deal with Governor Crittenden.

Crittenden

Bob Ford was able to get a meeting with the governor through his sister Martha Bolton, who had been the object of a gun battle with Bob and a man named Dick Liddil, which resulted in the death of Wood Hite. With Bolton's assistance, Bob Ford negotiated a deal with Crittenden, who told him that if James was killed, the reward money that had been put up by the railroads would belong to him. Crittenden also mentioned that if Ford happened to be the one to ensure that Jesse was killed, he had the authority to pardon him. Bob convinced Charley that they should kill Jesse and get the reward money. Incredibly, the governor of Missouri had conspired to murder Jesse James.

JESSE JAMES HOME

On the morning of April 3, 1882, Charley and Bob Ford were at Jesse's home in St. Joseph. Zee prepared breakfast for the men as Jesse got ready for a robbery that he had planned. Charley reportedly broke out into a sweat, causing Zee to comment and ask him if he was sick. Meanwhile, Jesse had taken off his gun belt to avoid drawing too much attention as he went in and out of his house. For Jesse to be without his guns was a rare occasion, but he gave the Fords the opening they had been waiting for. As Jesse climbed on to a chair to dust a picture, Bob and Charley drew their guns and approached him from behind. Bob shot Jesse point blank in the back of the head. Hearing the shot, Zee ran into the room and screamed, "You've killed him." Bob Ford's immediate response was, "I swear to God I didn't." His curious remark aside, Jesse James was dead.

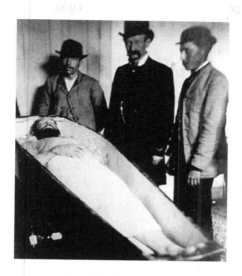

Jesse's body in a coffin

The Ford brothers surrendered to authorities and were convicted of murder, but Crittenden kept his word, and they were promptly pardoned and received some but not all of the $10,000 reward. However, the glory and notoriety they anticipated would come their way didn't materialize in the way they hoped. The Ford brothers initially billed themselves as the men who killed Jesse James and attempted to profit off of it by reenacting the murder and posing for photographs, but as was often the case in Jesse's lifetime, the public sided with him and was horrified at the cowardly way Bob Ford took Jesse's life. Bob was forced to leave Missouri in shame. Four years later, Charley Ford, done in by the stigma attached to what was called one of the most cowardly deeds in Missouri history, shot himself in the weeds near his home in Richmond, Missouri.

Bob Ford

At the behest of Jesse's mother, the inscription on Jesse's tombstone read, "Jesse W. James. Died April 3, 1882. Aged 34 years, 6 months, 28 days. Murdered by a traitor and a coward whose name is not worthy to appear here."

Chapter 7: Jesse James Lives On

Like many icons of the Wild West, much of the legend of Jesse James is wrapped up in myth. He lived in an era when Americans on the East Coast clamored for tales of the West, whether the tales were true or not. However, unlike some western icons that were tagged as being outlaws far more dangerous than they really were, Jesse James was built up to be a more chivalrous bandit than he was in real life. The fact is that Jesse James was a cold-blooded killer who did not, contrary to legend, steal from the rich to give to the poor. He robbed the rich and poor alike, all for his own personal gain.

It took very little time for Jesse's family to cash in on his name. His mother was offered $10,000 by a promoter for her son's body, presumably to put the deceased outlaw on public display. Zerelda gave it some consideration, but opted instead to have Jesse buried in her front yard where she could watch over his grave. When sightseers and the curious came by to visit Jesse's final resting place, Zerelda sold them pebbles from the gravesite for a few cents each. When she ran out of pebbles, she replenished her supply from the alley behind her house.

With the help of John Newman Edwards, Frank James surrendered to the governor of Missouri five months after Jesse died. He was jailed and tried for a robbery in Missouri and another in

Alabama but was acquitted of both crimes. Frank made some attempt to profit from the James family name when he and Cole Younger bought into the Buckskin Bill Wild West Show, and the name was even changed to the Cole Younger and Frank James Wild West Show in 1903. Some say that Frank had to quit due to poor health, while other historians say that the show was a disaster and they demanded that they be allowed to quit, with Younger resorting to pulling a gun on the owner to get the deal done. Either way, Frank eventually moved back to his family farm with his mother, where he gave tours for a quarter and sold picture postcards of his own likeness.

Zee James was offered money to write a book about her husband, but despite needing the money she refused to and would end up dying poor. Jesse's son did, though, writing, *Jesse James, My Father* in 1899. The first movie about Jesse appeared in 1908 when "The James Boys of Missouri" was released. The film was 18 minutes long, and taking into account that Jesse was still a sympathetic figure to many, the portrayal of him as an outlaw was done lightly. It was also a successful play for several years. This began a string of dozens of movie and television portrayals of Jesse or characters based on him that continued into the 21st century. Of all of the movies about him, Jesse's descendants claim that *The Assassination of Jesse James by the Coward Bob Ford*, starring Brad Pitt as Jesse in the last four months of his life, is the most accurate portrayal. The movie was adapted from a novel of the same name. Included in the film is the fact that Bob Ford went to New York to reenact the killing of Jesse James onstage, with his brother Charlie playing the role of Jesse.

In the wake of his notorious life and death, Jesse James was portrayed in several different was. Some viewed James as a symbol of resistance against government and industry, turning him into some sort of pre-Progressive Era rebel. Others viewed him as a symbol of the antebellum South whose life of crime was more about avenging the South and their lost way of life.

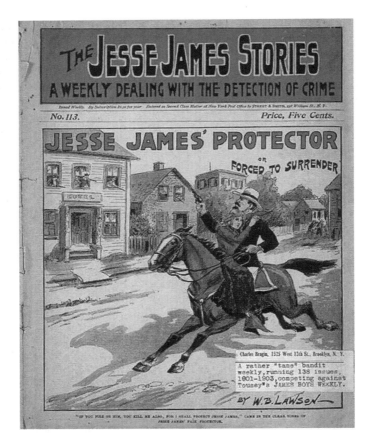

A 1901 dime novel about Jesse James

Jesse's name and likeness have been used to sell dime novels, comic books, and any number of collectibles. Items from lunch boxes to replica badges to shot glasses are highly desirable. Even reproductions of photographs of Jesse in a casket are easily found. In fact, the Jesse James Wax Museum in Stanton, Missouri offers tourists an array of Jesse James souvenirs, while keeping alive the debunked legend that Jesse faked his death and lived until 1948. Northfield, Minnesota has kept their link to Jesse's life alive with the Defeat of Jesse James Days festival, complete with a parade, an arts and crafts festival, and regular reenactments of the bank robbery.

It has taken time for some Americans to relinquish the image of Jesse James as a type of hero, which speaks to the deep wounds of the Civil War and the battle over the future of slavery as much as it does for Jesse's character. That Jesse lived and made his name as an outlaw during a time when there was such fascination with the West helped fuel his own need for attention and, in many respects, validation. Add into the mix the belief by those that sympathized with the Confederacy that he was a hero and the result is a legend.

However, that time has largely passed, and even as James remains perhaps the most famous outlaw of the West, glorified portrayals of him as heroic outlaw are now more about profiting off an interesting story than historical accuracy. New generations of Americans have come to view the antebellum South, the Civil War and the post-war bushwhacking much differently. In that context, Jesse James was hardly a hero, and despite his attempts to portray himself to the contrary, he was not a victim. He was caught up in an era of change and did not like the change he saw.

Despite this, James remains an important figure of American history, not because of the banks and railroads he robbed or the people he killed. The lesson is in his motives. He was not a rogue bandit, but a man who truly believed he was fighting for a righteous cause. He was far from the only one who felt that way in post-Civil War America. It is his link to America's past that makes Jesse James an important icon of the West.

Bibliography

Bell, Bob Boze. "Shoot-out at Hanska Slough." *True West Magazine*. August 6, 2012.

Drago, Harry Sinclair. *Outlaws on Horseback*. Lincoln, NE: University of Nebraska Press. 1998.

Murdoch, David H. *The American West: The Invention of a Myth*. Wales: Welsh Academic Press. 2001.

Yeatman, Ted P. *Frank and Jesse James: The Story Behind the Legend*. Nashville: Cumberland House Publishing, Inc. 2000.

Billy the Kid

Chapter 1: Henry McCarty's Early Years

"I wasn't the leader of any gang. I was for Billy all the time."

Very few facts about William Henry McCarty's life are indisputable, so it's only fitting that even his place and date of birth are up for debate. That's because no known records of his birth have survived, if they ever existed at all. Some say that Henry, as he was known, was born in the teeming slums of New York City on approximately November 23, 1859. Some even believe that William was not his first name, and that Billy the Kid may have been born Patrick McCarty, Michael McCarty, or Edward McCarty

What is known is that his mother was Catherine McCarty, a survivor of the Irish potato famine that swept over Ireland in the 1840s and left famine and disease in its wake. Like many of the Irish, Catherine sailed for the U.S., in search of a better life. It's unknown whether McCarty was Catherine's maiden name or whether she had taken that name upon marriage.

If Henry did begin his life in New York, the conditions there were better than Ireland, although not by much. The Irish neighborhoods, particularly the notorious Five Points and Mulberry Bend districts, were rampant with alcoholism, crime, disease, rats, and gang wars. This was also the era of William Tweed, best known as Boss Tweed, who was the head one of the most corrupt governmental regimes in New York City history. The Irish were an integral part of Tweed's strategy, as he openly bought their votes to stack the government with hand-chosen officials. Few Irish could turn away such easy money, and they naturally viewed Tweed as their hero. Corruption ruled New York for much of the latter stages of the 19th century, and with the crime that came with it, Catherine could not be blamed if she decided that New York was not the place for her or her children. It is known that she gave birth to another son, Joseph, but it has not been established if he was Henry's older or younger brother.

George Catlin's famous painting of the Five Points, 1827

Another possible location for Henry's birth is Indiana, based on the fact that the first recorded address for the McCartys is in Indianapolis. Next to Catherine's name in the Indianapolis City Directory for 1868 is the notation that she was the widow of Michael McCarty, who apparently was father to Henry and Joseph. Nothing definitive is known about Mr. McCarty, who had a fairly common name for the time, making it extremely difficult to pinpoint when and where he may have died.

More is known about William Henry Harrison Antrim from Huntsville, Indiana. Antrim was honorably discharged from the Union Army in October 1862 and returned to his native Indiana, where somewhere along the way he met Henry's mother. Some speculation is that he was a messenger for Merchant's Union Express and met the widow while delivering a package to her house. Antrim, 12 years younger than Catherine McCarty, started to court her soon after their meeting, becoming "Uncle Billy" to the McCarty boys.

The newly formed family left Indiana and went to Wichita, Kansas in the summer of 1870. Following the Civil War, Wichita was a rough and tumble frontier town that would soon experience a population boom due thanks to the railroad. Millions of cattle passed through

Wichita on the railroad on their way to the slaughterhouses north of Kansas. Less than a decade before, Wichita had been the Osage tribe territory. When Henry McCarty lived there, he saw a wide variety of characters from Indians to buffalo hunters to soldiers.

Life on this part of the prairie was not easy, and the weather extremes in Kansas presented their own challenges for people who lived in dugouts or wood cabins, as many did in Wichita. There was also very little work for a woman who did not plan to be a dance hall girl or a prostitute. Catherine McCarty had no intention of doing either of those things, but she was determined to give her sons a better life than she had in Ireland, so she opened a laundry service on Main Street.

As it turned out, business was brisk, and it helped McCarty and Antrim buy land on the outskirts of town. For $200, they bought just under 200 acres and cultivated seven of them for fruit trees. Antrim, likely with the help of the young McCarty boys, also built a house on the land, complete with a storm cellar. The location provided a bit of distance between Henry's family and the gambling, dancing, drinking, and violence of Wichita, but likely not enough to shield Henry from the lawlessness that was typical of cow towns of the era. Towns throughout the West walked a fine line between keeping some semblance of order while not disrupting the flow of cash into local saloons, gambling halls, and brothels.

Within about a year of arriving in Wichita, Catherine started showing signs of tuberculosis. It was a common killer of the 19th century and little could be done for those who had it. The dusty air of the prairie was not helpful to anyone with a persistent respiratory illness, which may have been the reason that Catherine uprooted her family from Wichita just when it seemed as if they were settling in. Those who could afford it, such as Western icon Doc Holliday, headed to the springs of Colorado and New Mexico. Those who could not afford the treatment at the springs settled for just being in the climate, which may have been the case for Catherine McCarty. Historians can only speculate, though, as her family's exact location between 1871 and early 1873 is unknown.

It is known that by 1873, Henry McCarty made his way to the state where he became known as Billy the Kid. That's because Catherine McCarty and William Antrim were married in the adobe brick First Presbyterian Church in Santa Fe on March 1, 1873. It is believed that Antrim's sister was living at the Exchange Hotel on the corner of the Santa Fe Plaza, and the family may have lived with her when they first arrived. Years later, locals claimed to have seen Henry washing dishes in the hotel kitchen and playing piano in the lobby. This would not be surprising because Henry always enjoyed music, an interest instilled in him by his mother. He also liked singing and dancing, which there was plenty of in New Mexico.

Furthermore, Henry had no trouble adapting to all aspects of his new surroundings and embracing the Mexican culture. He appreciated the spicy food and the colorful style of dress, especially the sombreros and beaded moccasins that he wore. Within months of arriving, he spoke Spanish like a native. These would all become hallmarks of Billy the Kid, and often the first things his contemporaries noticed about him.

Meanwhile, William Antrim, like many men of the era, was interested in striking it rich in the mines, and he soon moved the family to the southern region of New Mexico to the mining town of Silver City. For the first time in their lives, Henry and his brother, Josie, attended school when Dr. J. Webster opened the first public school in town on January 5, 1874. The town also hosted regular *bailes*, or dances, and when Catherine was feeling well enough, she and Henry attended them together. Henry moved easily when he danced and caught the eye of several young senoritas who were also there to dance the waltzes, polkas, or regional dances of the area. The locals recalled that Henry usually had a smile on his face.

Shortly after Henry started school, his mother's health began to deteriorate. She had experienced a reprieve from the debilitating cough, but it returned due to the smoke from the smelting furnaces of the silver mines. Catherine made a last-ditch attempt to buy herself more time and went to Hudson's Hot Springs for treatment. Mary Hudson, the owner's wife, became Catherine's friend and recalled how fond Catherine was of her boys. With his mother physically unable to supervise him and his stepfather spending more and more time away in the mines, Henry began to get into trouble. He and a friend devised a plan to steal costume jewelry from a local merchant and sell it in Mexico, but the plan was thwarted when Henry's friend became scared and told his father, who scolded both of the boys.

By the fall, Catherine was near death, and Clara Truesdell, who had graduated from nursing school in Chicago, took care of her every day. William Antrim was rarely home and, when Catherine died on September 16, 1874, he was not there, nor was he present for her funeral the next day. Before Catherine died, she asked Clara to watch out for her boys. Louis Abraham, who helped Henry and Josie dig their mother's grave in the town cemetery, would later say that he was glad she died without knowing the trouble that would come to her son.

At 14, Henry was for all intents and purposes an orphan. His stepfather was either unwilling or unable to care for his stepsons. Exactly what happened to Henry's brother Josie is unclear, but Antrim sold the family house and Henry spent some time living with the Truesdell family. He helped out in the kitchen of the hotel that the family owned to earn room and board and was reportedly one of the few boys that worked there that never stole anything. However, some sort of domestic disturbance resulted in Henry having to move out and into a boarding house.

Long after Henry was dead, with the myth of Billy the Kid on the rise, the stories about the murders and assorted other crimes that he was supposedly responsible for in Grant County grew.

Whether it was killing a kitten with his pocketknife or stoning a Chinese man to death, Billy the Kid often got the blame. Much, if not all of it, was either greatly exaggerated or simply a lie. It may have helped sell dime novels or newspapers if Billy the Kid was linked to a crime, but in many cases, it simply was not true.

It is true, though, that Henry made the acquaintance of a petty thief named George Schaefer while staying at the boarding house in Silver City. Schaefer, nicknamed Sombrero Jack, liked Henry and let him tag along with him in the saloons and gambling halls. Likely eager for a parental figure, Henry willingly followed Sombrero Jack's lead, including his plan to rob Charlie Sun's laundry service. Sun was a Chinese immigrant who was also a regular target of taunting and harassment by the local boys.

On September 4, 1875, Henry served as the lookout while Sombrero Jack stole blankets, clothes, and two loaded revolvers from Sun's laundry. Sombrero Jack stowed some of the goods in a pit in nearby Georgetown, then offered Henry some of a share of it in exchange for smuggling it all back into Silver City. When the boarding house owner was cleaning Henry's room a few days later, she found the stolen property, which included one of the guns, and called Sheriff Harvey Whitehill.

Whitehill was aware that Henry didn't have parents to watch over him, but he had previously detained Henry for stealing cheese and now wanted to teach him a lesson. Thus, Whitehill arrested him on the spot. Chances are, he was only going to let Henry sit in the jailhouse for a day or two to think about what he had done, then take him home since his wife told him to bring the boy home for breakfast. He didn't get the chance, though, because after two days in jail, on September 25, Henry escaped. Using his powers of persuasion, a guard allowed Henry to spend some time in the jailhouse corridor, out of his cell. After being left alone for about 20 minutes, a man who had been standing nearby confirmed that he saw the skinny teenager climb out of the chimney. Henry was now a wanted man.

When Billy the Kid became a household name, the legend became that he had fled Silver City because he had killed a man there. That legend was refuted by Whitehill, who later wrote an account of his time as a frontier law man in Silver City. Whitehill wrote about the two offenses Billy the Kid was arrested for, while also noting he was an affable kid who had participated in the crimes more out of a necessity than because he was a hard criminal. According to Whitehill, the kill The Kid was credited with by the rumors were completely baseless.

Chapter 2: Henry McCarty on the Run

"Billy never talked much of the past. He was always looking into the future." – Frank Coe

Not surprisingly, the legends surrounding what happened next are just as colorful. One story said that Henry made it to Camp Thomas in Arizona territory, where he shot and killed a buffalo soldier with a shotgun, then took off on a stolen horse. Given that Camp Thomas did not exist yet, that story is not true. There are also other wild tales of Billy the Kid roaming the country, slaughtering Indians and brawling in New York City. The most likely story is that he got help from Clara Truesdell, the closet thing that Henry had to a mother at the time. Chauncey Truesdell said that his mother washed and dried Henry's clothes and gave him food. After he spent the night on the floor, Mrs. Truesdell put Henry on a stagecoach to Clifton, a mining town in the mountains of southeast Arizona.

Clifton was named for Henry Clifton, a prospector who made his way to Southern Arizona from Prescott to mine for gold and instead found copper ore. This Henry was not there to mine, though. He went to Clifton to find his stepfather, but when he found William and told him the story, Antrim refused to help. With nothing left to do, Henry stole clothes and a gun from his stepfather's room and never saw him again.

Over the next two years, Henry bounced from place to place in Arizona, perhaps earning money at a cattle ranch or the gambling halls. In the spring of 1876, Henry heard that there was better opportunity to make money off of the soldiers at the card tables in Camp Grant, north of Tucson. Using a horse he stole from a soldier at Camp Goodwin, Henry left for Fort Grant.

Fort Grant in the late 19th century

At Fort Grant, Henry began to make a name for himself as gambler and an outlaw who was particularly adept at stealing horses. He started to wear a pinky ring, which many superstitious gamblers wore for luck, and he dressed in brightly colored scarves. When he earned enough money, he bought a six-shooter. For most men of the West, a gun was a necessity, but it was even truer for the teenager that now was called Kid Antrim, a playful reference to his small physique and lack of facial hair. Indeed, Kid Antrim was smaller than most of the men he encountered and needed an equalizer.

It seems Kid Antrim's first opportunity to use his six-shooter came on August 17, 1877 when he crossed paths with a bully named Windy Cahill. Taking note of Henry's small stature, Cahill amused himself by slapping Henry around until he had him down on the ground. Henry yelled for Cahill to let him up, but he wouldn't, so Henry freed his arm and reached for his holster. He fired his gun into Cahill's stomach. He may have been able to make a case of self-defense, but not wanting to take the chance, Henry took off, leaving Cahill to die later that night.

On the run again, Henry changed his name to one of his most notorious monikers, William H. Bonney. Henry was now Billy. He rode a stolen horse out of Arizona and back to New Mexico. He survived the harsh late summer heat with the help of Mexican ranchers out in the open range, who took him in and gave him a meal when he needed to eat. Mexicans had owned land in New Mexico for generations, but an influx of British and Irish immigrants was changing that. Like many, they viewed the West as the land of opportunity and came to the United States with money to spend. They invested in railroads, mining, and cattle ranches, but what they really wanted was land. With the assistance of corrupt bankers and an equally corrupt law enforcement system, many wealthy immigrants were able to take the land right out from under the Mexicans.

Such was the case with Lawrence Murphy and James Dolan. In Fort Stanton, New Mexico in 1866, Murphy went into business with Emil Fritz and the two men opened L.G. Murphy & Co., a store and brewery. Through government contracts, the company became the supplier of vegetables and meat to Fort Stanton and the Mescalero-Apache Reservation. Murphy and Fritz then sold land that they did not really own to local farmers. When farmers were not able to pay back their loans, Murphy and Fritz foreclosed on the land and took the cattle and crops. They then turned around and used the cattle and crops to fulfill the obligations of their government contracts. A group of local politicians from Santa Fe, known as "The Ring," were in on the scheme and made sure that Murphy and Fritz did not have to worry about legal problems.

The good times at Fort Stanton came to an end for Murphy and Fritz in September 1873. Murphy had hired a fiery-tempered James Dolan, another Irishman, to work as a clerk in the store. Dolan got into a conflict with a local soldier and tried to shoot and kill him. With complaints about price gouging and shorting the Indians on supply orders already circulating, L.G. Murphy & Co. was evicted from Fort Stanton. Meanwhile, Fritz sold his interest in the company to Murphy and returned to Germany after being diagnosed with kidney disease.

However, the government contracts remained intact, allowing Murphy to build a new store in Lincoln County. Dolan bought into the business in 1874, and Murphy and Dolan Mercantile and Banking soon had a stranglehold on the economy of Lincoln County. The large two-story building, which became the Lincoln County Courthouse in 1930, was nicknamed "The House," which also came to reference Murphy, Dolan, and their crew of corrupt politicians and members of law enforcement. Now working with Fort Sumner, The House picked up right where it left off in Fort Stanton, investing in railroads, cattle, and land. If a business transaction occurred in Lincoln County, it is highly likely that Murphy and Dolan were involved.

Murphy was also an alcoholic, drinking to the point that he was not a factor in the war that was developing between the Irish and British in Lincoln County. In March 1877, the face of the business changed when Murphy was diagnosed with colon cancer. The worse the pain got, the more Murphy drank. Murphy and Dolan had already taken on a new business partner, John Riley, in the fall. With Murphy facing terminal illness, he sold his stake in the company to Dolan and Riley and the business changed to Jas. J. Dolan & Co. Lawrence Murphy spent the last year of his life getting treatment for cancer in Santa Fe.

Chapter 3: William H. Bonney Enters the Lincoln County War

"At least two-hundred men have been killed in Lincoln County during the past three years, but I did not kill all of them." – Billy the Kid

It was about this same time that Billy arrived in town. He had joined forces with a gang of ex-soldiers and assorted desperadoes at an abandoned army post called Apache Tejo, south of Silver City. Former cavalry sergeant John Kinney was the boss of the gang, called The Boys, but the leader of the pack was Jesse Evans. Under his lead, The Boys stole cattle, horses, or whatever else Kinney needed to make a profit. As much as Billy the Kid came to be known as a notorious outlaw, Evans was much more feared during his lifetime. The Boys would not hesitate to kill anyone who got in their way. It was also understood that the gang was on the secret payroll of Dolan and Company, stealing horses and providing guns for hire to The House.

Jesse Evans

New Mexico was the site of a brutal land war between the English and the Irish, and Billy the Kid now found himself right in the middle of it. Lincoln County was the largest county in the entire country, covering about a quarter of the state, and it was rampant with greed and corruption. Disputes were settled with guns, and most of the gunmen were never punished. Much of the land was either unsurveyed public land or the product of Spanish land grants, issued years before white men entered the territory. Its remote location also contributed to the lawlessness of the region. Despite its sparse population, New Mexico accounted for 15 percent of the murders in the United States in the 1870s. The Civil War had made many men immune to the horrors of death.

Early 1877 not only brought Billy to Lincoln County, but it also brought competition to The House. A trio comprised of Alexander McSween from Scotland, John Tunstall from England, and John Chisum from Texas formed an alliance with the goal of creating their own financial empire. They established their own bank and store not far from The House; clearly, the Irishmen did not intimidate Tunstall. He wrote a letter to his father in England in April 1877 and explained that in order to succeed in New Mexico, a man needed to be part of "a ring." He was building his own ring and it was his intention to "get half of every dollar that is made in the county by anyone."[16] He set his goal as three years, but within a year, both he and McSween would be dead.

Billy's first encounter with Tunstall was shortly after he stole his horses in 1877 in Rio Feliz, about 30 miles south of Lincoln County. He was put into the earthen pit that served as the county jail, but instead of pressing charges against him, Tunstall offered Billy an opportunity to work for him instead. The "ring" that he told his father about needed men like the Kid and the Kid was grateful to get out of jail, so he accepted.

Tunstall was far from a saint. After all, he was trying to do the same thing that Dolan was doing. However, he treated his men well, and the Kid felt loyal to him. He said that Tunstall was the only one that treated him like a decent human being. For the first time in a long time, Billy had steady work, a place to sleep, and regular meals. As was typical for him, he was attracted to any semblance of a home that he could find.

Early in 1878, Tunstall and McSween ran into money problems, brought on by a civil suit for $10,000 filed by The House. William Brady was the first sheriff of Lincoln County, and though he proved himself to be a capable lawman, he was also close to his fellow Irishman and also deeply in debt to them. When it came time to issue a fake court order for the livestock from Tunstall's ranch, it was Brady who gladly led a posse to ride out to the ranch to issue the order.

The bad blood that boiled between the Irish and the British in Europe now carried over to the wide-open spaces of New Mexico. Survivors of the Irish potato famine would have no mercy on a Brit. Irish Catholics were not allowed, under British rule, to purchase land. They were permitted only to rent small plots of land from the British and most Irish peasants chose to grow potatoes because they could grow three times as many potatoes as grain on their small plots. One acre of potatoes could feed a family for a year. However, in 1845, fungus devastated most of the potato crops and with the British slow to provide relief, nearly a million Irish starved and died from disease. Two million others were forced to emigrate to Great Britain, the U.S., and Canada, just as Catherine McCarty did. The House was not going to allow an Englishman to take what they worked so hard to get.

---

[16] Wallis, Michael. *Billy the Kid: Endless Ride*. Page 179.

On February 18, 1878, Tunstall rounded a group of his men, including the Kid, to ride into town to challenge the claim on his property. Along the way, he saw Brady and his posse, and thinking this was a chance to discuss the situation, rode up to Brady. His men, meanwhile, were chasing a flock of wild turkey, leaving Tunstall alone. Tunstall's men yelled for Tunstall to take cover when they saw Buck Morton point his shotgun at him and shoot him in the chest before he could even get out of the saddle. Another of Brady's posse, Tom Hill then walked over to Tunstall as he lay bleeding in the dirt, took his pistol, and shot him in the back of the head. An investigator later implicated Jesse Evans in the shooting as well. The final move was to shoot Tunstall's horse. Brady's men covered Tunstall with a blanket and put his bloody topcoat under his head, as if for a pillow. They put Tunstall's hat under the horse's head.

The Kid and the rest of Tunstall's men watched horrified from the cover of the nearby rocks and trees. When Tunstall's body was laid out in McSween's parlor, Billy approached the dead man and said, "I'll get some of them before I die." McSween was a lawyer, though, and wanted to take a lawful approach to getting revenge for his partner's death. Knowing that most of law enforcement was on The House's payroll, McSween obtained an arrest warrant for Sheriff Brady and his posse from the justice of the peace, John B. Wilson.

The Kid and Fred Waite were deputized, and along with Constable Atanacio Martinez, who was not very eager to be party to arresting Sheriff Brady, went to Dolan's store to serve the warrants. Brady and other associates of The House greeted them, guns drawn. Instead of arresting Brady and his crew, Billy and his men were taken at gunpoint to the county jail, where they remained until after Tunstall's funeral.

McSween tried to enlist the help of authorities to investigate not only the murder of Tunstall, but also what amounted to an organized crime syndicate led by Dolan. However, when one of the Kid's friends, Rob Widenmann, claimed that Dolan tried to have him poisoned, it merely added fuel to the fire, and it was evident that the violence was not about to end. Under investigation for embezzlement anyway – charges of which he was later cleared - McSween wrote his will and took off to the mountains with his wife.

With McSween on the run, Squire Wilson appointed Dick Brewer, Tunstall's foreman, as a "special constable" with the authority to make arrests. Brewer formed a posse, the Regulators, which included the Kid, Charlie Bowdre, and several other men, including some Mexican-Americans who wanted to fight The House. At times, the Regulators had as many as 60 men under its umbrella. Acting as a lawfully appointed posse, the Regulators operated for five months with the sole intent of avenging the death of John Tunstall. Many claimed that of all of the Regulators, the Kid was the most loyal and he was present for every gunbattle that took place.

In March 1878, about one month after Tunstall's murder, the Regulators found Buck Morton, the man who shot Tunstall out of his saddle, and two other men. It's been claimed that Morton surrendered only on the condition that his captors would promise to bring him back alive to Lincoln. Dick Brewer assured the prisoners they would reach Lincoln alive, and when other members of the posse argued in favor of killing them, one of the Regulators, William McCloskey, argued against it.

3 days later, on March 9, 1878, Morton, Baker and William McCloskey were all dead. It's been assumed that they were shot because the Regulators assumed if they took the men to Sheriff Brady he would just let them go. The Regulators insisted that Morton and Baker had tried to escape and shot McCloskey in the process, but most were skeptical that Morton would shoot his one friend. They also figured it was no coincidence that Morton and Baker had been shot 11 times, once for each Regulator in the posse. On top of that, Tom Hill and Jesse Evans, who had also been part of Tunstall's murder, were also shot while trying to steal sheep. Hill died and Evans was badly wounded.

While the vigilante justice was carrying itself out on March 9, on that same day Governor Samuel Axtell rode into Lincoln County to investigate, per the request of Brady, who described the situation in Lincoln County as "anarchy." Federal troops from Fort Stanton were put on alert, and Axtell cancelled Squire Wilson's appointment as justice of the peace and revoked Widenmann's duties as deputy marshal. By doing so, he removed any legal authority that the Regulators had, turning them into a band of outlaw vigilantes.

Late in the evening of March 31, the Regulators launched their plan to get Brady. The Kid and five other men snuck into town and hid behind an adobe wall in a corral near Tunstall's store. The next morning, as Brady left the Dolan store, the Regulators unleashed at least a dozen rounds of gunfire and killed him in the muddy street. A deputy was also killed. For unknown reasons, the Kid and another man named Jim French ran to Brady's body, perhaps looking for warrants or a gun. A shot came from a nearby house and went through the Kid's thigh and into French's leg, but they were both able to escape.

Sheriff Brady

With the cold-blooded assassination of their sheriff, the Regulators lost sympathy from many in the town. They were now viewed as murderers and no better than The House. The Regulators went back to San Patricio, the tiny community on the Ruidoso River that served as their headquarters. The Kid and French recovered from their wounds, and the Regulators picked up new men to join the crew before moving up the river and into the mountains on April 4. Their destination was Blazer's Mill, located on the Mescalero Apache Indian Reservation in the Tularosa Creek canyon. The Regulators heard that men who were involved in Tunstall's murder were there and Brewer planned to serve his arrest warrants, whether they were valid or not.

The small settlement called Blazer's Mill belonged to a dentist named Joseph Blazer, who leased a two-story adobe house to the federal government, where Indian agent Frederick Godfroy and his wife lived. The Godfroys took in lodgers and Mrs. Godfroy ran a small restaurant, known for its hearty meals. While the Regulators were enjoying the hot meal, Buckshot Roberts rode into town, possibly to see if a check he was waiting for had arrived. Roberts wanted no more to do with the Lincoln County War and was in the process of selling his ranch. He also had ridden in the posse that killed Tunstall.

When the Regulators spotted Roberts, it left neither side with very little choice of what to do. If the Regulators simply left, Roberts would chase them down and shoot them. If Roberts tried to leave, the Regulators would kill him. Frank Coe, one of the Regulators who knew Roberts the best, tried to talk him into surrendering, but Roberts would not agree to that.

Meanwhile, Dick Brewer grew impatient and led his posse, including the Kid, out of the dining room, and toward Roberts and Coe. Both Roberts and Charlie Bowdre fired simultaneously, touching off the gunfight. Roberts was almost immediately shot in the stomach, a mortal wound, but he managed to keep firing from his Winchester at the Regulators as he headed for the doorway of Blazer's house. In the process, Middleton was hit in the chest, Frank Coe's cousin George had his trigger finger blown off, and Doc Scurlock had a graze wound. When Billy the Kid realized Roberts had fired all his bullets, he ran up to kill Roberts, only to be beaten unconscious by the barrel of Roberts' gun.

Roberts managed to get into the house and barricade himself, now using another rifle that belonged to Blazer to keep shooting. The Regulators, however, were stunned by the carnage that had been inflicted by Roberts. As most of the posse began to care for their own, Brewer moved around the house and started firing into the room in which Roberts was laying down. Seeing the smoke from Brewer's gun rising behind the log pile Brewer was hiding behind, Roberts waited for Brewer to stick his head out. As soon as Brewer did, Roberts let off a shot that hit Brewer in the eye and tore off much of his head with it.

The Regulators were stunned by the bloodshed and the loss of their leader. Gathering up their wounded, they left Roberts behind, who died a painful death the next day. Ironically, Roberts and Brewer were buried side by side.

The gunfight at Blazer's Mill only served to further tarnish the image of the Regulators; some felt that Roberts had been ambushed and appreciated how he continued to battle despite his fatal wounds. The Regulators went back to San Patricio to plot their next move. In the spring, a grand jury handed down indictments in the Tunstall murder, as well as indictments in the killings of Brady, his deputy, and Roberts. William H. Bonney was one of the men wanted for the murder of Sheriff Brady and Buckshot Roberts.

George Coe in later years, clearly missing his trigger finger

Chapter 4: The End of the Lincoln County War

With Brewer dead, the Regulators elected Frank McNab, a former cattle detective, as their new leader. Meanwhile, John Copeland was appointed the new sheriff to replace Brady, which was a bit of a stroke of luck for the Regulators since he was friendlier to them than The House. The new sheriff was often seen out in the saloons and gambling halls with the Regulators, never getting around to serving the warrants that he had for their arrest. McSween also returned to town when the embezzlement charges were dismissed.

During this time, the Kid preferred to go to McSween's house instead of the saloon. On many nights, Mary Early, the preacher's wife, played the piano in McSween's parlor, and the Kid liked to go there and sing. Early recalled that the Kid and any of the other Regulators that joined him sang with enthusiasm, "They stood behind me with their guns and belts full of cartridges; I suppose I was off tune as often as on it as I felt very nervous, though they were nice and polite."[17]

On April 29, 1878, the Seven Rivers Posse, Dolan's new posse, headed to Lincoln to join up with Dolan's other men. The group stopped for a break at the Charles Fritz Ranch on the Rio Bonito, about nine miles out of town. The Fritz family passed the word that Frank Coe, McNab, and another of the Regulators, Ab Saunders, would be by that day to get water for their horses. The posse waited and they shot at the Regulators as they passed by on their way to the spring. When it was over, McNab was dead, Saunders was wounded and captured, and Coe's horse was killed, forcing him to surrender. Coe was taken to Dolan's store when the posse rode back into town.

When word got back to the Regulators about the new posse, they scattered throughout the town. Another gunbattle broke out, allowing Frank Coe to simply walk back to his crew. Sheriff Copland had had enough and finally called out the army for assistance. Buffalo soldiers were sent into Lincoln with orders to arrest anyone involved in the war, resulting in the arrest of 30 men, who were taken back to Fort Stanton. Copland asked that the men be remanded to his custody, but when the men were released to him, he could do nothing other than to order them to stop fighting.

However, neither side was willing to quit yet. By early May 1878, the Regulators had replaced yet another killed leader, this time with Josiah "Doc" Shurlock, who was deputized by Sheriff Copland. Meanwhile, the partnership between Dolan and Riley was also in the process of formally ending. On May 14, a group of Mexican-American and white riders, with Scurlock and Josefita Chavez in the lead, swept into the Seven Rivers area and overtook a camp of Dolan's men, killing their cook, Manuel "Indian" Segovia. Two of Dolan's men were also wounded but managed to escape. The Regulators also took a couple dozen of the horses and mules from the camp and set the cattle free.

What the Regulators did not realize was that the cattle and horses did not belong to Dolan and Riley anymore. They were the property of Tom "Boss" Catron, one of the most powerful men in the region, who was not at all pleased about his cattle being scattered into the plains. He sent an angry letter to Governor Axtell insisting that law and order be restored. He also pointed out that the sheriff was friendly with the Regulators. Even though he had no authority to do so, Axtell removed Copland as sheriff and hand-selected George Peppin.

As with any war, both sides spent their last weeks trying to get in as many shots and take as many casualties as possible before the war inevitably had to end. Such was the case with the Lincoln County War, which continued with a barrage of gunfights and bloodshed into the

---

[17] Wallis, Michael. *Billy the Kid: Endless Ride.* Pages 204 – 205.

summer of 1878. Unfortunately for Peppin, Congress had recently passed the Posse Comitatus Act, forbidding military intervention in civil disturbances unless authorized by an act of Congress or the Constitution. However, in violation of the act, Colonel Nathan Dudley intervened in Lincoln County on July 19, bringing with him a howitzer and a Gatling gun with 2,000 rounds of ammunition.

At this point, many of the Regulators left town, while those that remained holed up in McSween's house. When they refused to surrender, Peppin set the house on fire, and as the fire burned into the night, the Regulators and the McSweens plotted their escapes. McSween finally agreed to surrender, but as he walked toward his yard, his body was hit with several bullets and he was killed. Dolan's posse had won. As their crowning achievement, they made two of McSween's grief-stricken men play their fiddles as they cried, while the victorious Dolan crew danced around the dead bodies and fired their guns into the air. Others ran for Lincoln's only street and looted Tunstall's store. The war was over, but the corruption continued on.

What remained of the Regulators now used Fort Sumner as their home base. The exact movements of the Kid during this time are not known, but several of the Regulators quit and he became the new leader. With the Kid in the lead, they stole horses and 150 head of cattle from the Fritz ranch, the site of Frank McNab's murder, and moved on toward the town of Tacosa in the Texas Panhandle. The town was a popular cattle stop and trading center, as well as a good place to unload stolen cattle. Billy's loyal friend, Tom O'Folliard, was likely with him throughout these times.

It was here that the Kid met a young doctor named Henry Hoyt, who also became a close friend. Hoyt confirmed years later that the Kid was active in horse trading, gambling, and target shooting, but he apparently did not like whiskey. He was only in the saloons so he could gamble. Many times, Hoyt encouraged the Kid to take off for Mexico or South America, where he could blend in and start a fresh life, but the Kid refused. Tacosa suited him well as a temporary stop-off, with its weekly dances and pretty senoritas in festive dresses.

The woman he really loved, though, was Paulita Maxwell, the younger sister of Pete Maxwell in Fort Sumner. Pete was the son of Lucien B. Maxwell, a rich land baron who bought the abandoned military fort and developed it into a town. Pete was not happy about his sister's relationship with the Kid, and unfortunately for the Kid, he also happened to be friends with Pat Garret, who the Kid would soon come to know all too well.

When the Regulators officially disbanded, the Kid and O'Folliard were regularly seen about town in Fort Sumner. Things had changed since they were in Texas, though. President Rutherford B. Hayes, tired of the chaos in New Mexico, fired Samuel Axtell and appointed Civil War veteran Lew Wallace as governor. Wallace had a controversial Civil War career due to the battle of Shiloh, and he later became best known for the novel *Ben-Hur*, but now he found himself trying to sort out a mess in the Southwest. One of Wallace's first actions as governor was to issue a statement that he would grant amnesty to anyone involved in the Lincoln County War, assuming they were not already under criminal indictment. On December 22, 1878, the Kid and O'Folliard turned themselves in for the purpose of getting a proclamation of amnesty from Wallace, but the Kid was facing two murder indictments and was not eligible for amnesty. After a few hours, figuring they might have inadvertently placed themselves in a predicament, the Kid and O'Folliard walked out and fled.

Lew Wallace

It is not exactly clear what made the Kid decide to try and make peace with his enemies, but on February 18, 1879, a year to the day of Tunstall's murder, the Kid and some of his friends went to Lincoln to meet James Dolan and his men. Upon the Kid's arrival, Jesse Evans suggested to Dolan and his men that they should shoot the Kid, to which he allegedly responded, "I don't care to open negotiations with a fight, but if you'll come at me three at a time, I'll whip the whole damned bunch of you!"

Whether or not that's true, it seemed the famous adversaries eventually reached a truce, and everyone except the Kid sealed the deal with several shots of whiskey. However, the Kid became alarmed when he witnessed the drunken group of men shoot and kill Huston Chapman. The man, who only had one arm, was a successful attorney and had taken Susan McSween's case in the murder of her husband, making him a sworn enemy of Dolan's crew. Even though there is nothing to suggest that he was involved, the Kid was now associated with another murder.

Governor Wallace ordered that anyone involved in Chapman's murder be arrested. On March 13, 1879, he received a letter from the Kid offering information about Chapman's murder in exchange for amnesty. The governor agreed, but told the Kid that he had to be willing to be part of a "fake arrest." Wallace said that if the Kid complied, "I will let you go scot free with a pardon in your pockets for all your misdeeds."[18] After ensuring that O'Folliard was part of the deal, the Kid agreed.

Thus, that March Billy the Kid met Governor Wallace in person, allegedly with his revolver in one hand and a Winchester rifle in the other. The deal called for the Kid to stay in the Lincoln County jail for a bit before testifying, and during his short stay, the Kid scrawled on one of the prison's wooden doors, "William Bonney was incarcerated here first time December 22, 1878; second time March 21st, 1879, and hope I never will be again." Wallace was baffled when local minstrels serenaded the Kid as he and O'Folliard played cards with their guards, and he described the scene in a letter to Secretary of the Interior Carl Schurz, "A precious specimen named 'The Kid,' whom the sheriff is holding here in the Plaza, as it is called, is an object of tender regard. I heard singing and music the other night; going to the door, I found the minstrels of the village actually serenading the fellow in his prison."

Billy the Kid's testimony was used to indict John Dolan, but the District Attorney himself was affiliated with The House, and he refused to set the Kid free after his testimony. Eventually, the Kid was put under house arrest in Lincoln in the home of Juan Patron.

Chapter 5: Criminal Indictments against William H. Bonney

Over 200 criminal indictments were filed against 50 men involved in the Lincoln County War. Most had the charges dropped or they just disappeared, but this was not the case for the Kid, who appeared to be the scapegoat that the men who were actually responsible for the war needed. District Attorney William Rynerson, a colleague of James Dolan, had no intention of letting the Kid get away unscathed, and it seems unlikely that Wallace ever intended to honor his deal with the Kid. Wallace later told a reporter that he was not sure why the Kid would expect clemency from him. The Kid would write a letter complaining to Wallace, "I have done everything that I promised you I would and you have done nothing that you promised me." Ultimately, the only man to ever be tried and convicted for crimes committed during the Lincoln County War was none other than William H. Bonney. While this no doubt annoyed the Kid, Dolan and his group's attempt to paint him as one of the large instigators of the Lincoln County war eventually had the side-effect of making him a legendary frontier outlaw, as the Kid would be credited for much of

---

[18] Wallis, Michael, *Billy the Kid: Endless Ride.* Page 179.

the war's violence, even though he personally perpetrated little of it.

The Kid ran away before he could be taken into custody, but once again, rather than disappearing into Mexico, he went to Las Vegas, New Mexico to earn some money at the gaming tables. In early 1880, Billy the Kid would have one of the most famous run-ins of his life. That January, the Kid was at a saloon in Fort Sumner when a Texan named Joe Grant loudly bragged he would kill Billy the Kid if he ever encountered him. According to legend, the Kid asked to see Grant's gun, and rotated the gun's cylinders so that the hammer would fall on an empty chamber the first time Grant pulled the trigger. After telling Grant he was the Kid, the drunken Grant fired his revolver, only to have the hammer fall on an empty chamber. The Kid then responded with a shot to the chin, instantly killing him. The Kid would later famously claim of the Grant shooting, "It was a game for two, and I got there first."

Other variations of the Grant story have popped up, but all of them involve the Kid making sure the next shot was an empty chamber. In one telling of the story, the Kid's back was turned, and when he heard the click of the dry fire of the gun, he whirled around and shot the man.

It was also at some point during this time that he posed for a ferrotype photo in Fort Sumner, the only authenticated photo of him that exists.

In November 1880, the handsome and tall Pat Garrett was elected sheriff of Lincoln County. Later that month, Garrett tracked the Kid down at the Greathouse-Kuch ranch and when Jim Carlyle, a blacksmith who was a member of Garrett's posse, was killed, the Kid was implicated again, although he denied it. The negative publicity against the Kid grew and, for the first time, he was referred to in print at "Billy the Kid," which only added to his notorious outlaw image. The Kid again reached out to Governor Wallace to insist that the way he was being portrayed was inaccurate, but Wallace not only ignored him, he issued a bounty on his head: $500 for the capture of Billy the Kid.

Pat Garrett

Promising a $500 reward stepped up the manhunt and newspapers gave accounts of every movement of Garrett's Panhandle Posse. Garrett caught up with the Kid again on December 19, 1880, ambushing his group in Fort Sumner. O'Folliard was killed in the ambush, but the Kid, now devastated at the loss of his friend, made it to a one-room stone house at Stinking Springs with four other men. On December 23, Garrett, acting on a tip, surrounded the house and unleashed a hail of gunfire, thinking he had just seen the Kid come out. The person he actually saw and killed was Charlie Bowdre, who had come outside to feed his horse. Garrett then shot the horse so that its body would block the doorway and serve as a barricade.

Garrett and his group now waited out Billy the Kid and the remaining outlaws inside, and though legends that Garrett and the Kid were friends are inaccurate, the two engaged in a playful banter during the siege. Once Garrett's group started cooking food, Garrett invited the Kid to come out to eat, while the Kid replied by inviting Garrett to "go to hell". Finally, out of food and options, the outlaws surrendered and were allowed to eat along with Garrett's group. Upon surrendering, the Kid allegedly said to Garrett, "'Pat, you son-of-a-bitch, they told me there was a hundred Texans here from the Canadian River! If I'd a-known there wasn't no more than this, you'd never have got me!"

Garrett took the Kid into custody to much fanfare in New Mexico, making himself a hero. Reporters swarmed the Kid and were surprised to see that he did not act like the cold-blooded killer that they expected. The Kid even said to one of the reporters, "'Advise persons never to engage in killing." Miguel Antonio Otero was the governor of New Mexico Territory between 1897 and 1907 and a lawyer in 1880. He recalled meeting the Kid in Las Vegas, where he was in shackles waiting to go to Santa Fe for his murder trial. Otero said, "I liked the Kid very much. Nothing would have pleased me more than to have witnessed his escape."[19]

Chapter 6: The Death of Billy the Kid

"People thought me bad before, but if ever I should get free, I'll let them know what bad means." – Billy the Kid to a reporter from the Daily New Mexican after his capture at Stinking Springs.

After being arrested by Garrett, the Kid was taken from Fort Sumner to Las Vegas, New Mexico, where he was also given a chance to speak to reporters. The Kid was apparently playful, as he mentioned to one reporter, "What's the use of looking on the gloomy side of everything? The laugh's on me this time. Is the jail at Santa Fe any better than this? This is a terrible place to put a fellow in." The question about Santa Fe was made in reference to the fact that the Kid was on his way there next, and while he was imprisoned there for the next three months he asked Lew Wallace for clemency. Not surprisingly, Wallace didn't oblige, telling the Las Vegas Gazette, "I can't see how a fellow like him should expect any clemency from me."

The charges in the Roberts killing were dropped, but the Kid was found guilty of Brady's murder and was sentenced to hang on May 13, 1881. The Kid offered no words in his defense. With that, he was taken to jail in Lincoln, where he was regularly taunted by Bob Ollinger, who, along with Deputy James Bell, was ordered to guard his cell. Ollinger blamed the Kid for the death of his friend, Bob Beckwith, and never let him forget it.

---

[19] Wallis, Michael. *Billy the Kid: Endless Ride.* Page 227.

The Lincoln County Jail

On April 28, with Garrett away, the Kid somehow got out his cell and managed to arm himself. Some suggest that he asked to use the outhouse behind the courthouse and a friend planted a gun for him nearby. At any rate, the Kid swung his heavy handcuffs at Bell, then maneuvered a gun into position and shot and killed Bell, who fell into the courthouse yard. As someone ran for help, the Kid grabbed Ollinger's shotgun from Garrett's office. When Ollinger approached the building, the Kid pointed the gun out the open window, said, "Hello Bob!" and blasted Ollinger's body with buckshot, killing him instantly. The Kid then forced the cook at gunpoint to get a pickax and remove his shackles. From the courthouse balcony, the Kid shouted to the growing crowd that he had not meant to kill Bell, but he would kill anyone that tried to prevent his escape. When the Kid took off on the deputy clerk's horse, some say he was singing. The same horse, now without its famous rider, came back into town two days later.

After this most daring escape, it would have surprised nobody if he had finally left the country. Instead, 3 months later the rumor was that the Kid hadn't gone far at all; in fact, the story was that the Kid was back in the Fort Sumner area, around where he had been captured in December. Nobody was more surprised than Pat Garrett that the Kid, once again, did not leave the area. Perhaps it was because Paulita Maxwell was pregnant, which could explain why the Kid ended up in the Maxwell house. Garrett had heard that the Kid was in Fort Sumner but didn't believe it at first. Finally, when Pete Maxwell confirmed it, Garrett rode out to the Maxwell house on July 14, 1881.

Shortly after 9:00 p.m. that summer evening, Garrett and two of his men waited for the Kid in a peach orchard. After midnight, they approached the house. It was dark and the Kid was without a hat and boots. In his stocking feet, he walked toward the porch, on his way to cut some meat from a freshly slaughtered deer hanging on the Maxwell's porch. The Kid saw men in the dark and drew his gun from his waistband. "Quien es?" he said, asking in Spanish, "Who is it?" He repeated the question in English and Maxwell said to Garrett, "El es", meaning "It's him." Garrett fired twice and 21 year old Billy the Kid was dead.

Naturally, there have been countless variations of the events of that night, some portraying Garrett as acting in self-defense, others making him out to be a murderer. One account had Garrett talking to Maxwell, a friend of the Kid's, when the Kid entered the room to their surprise. One theory even goes so far as to claim Garrett bound and gagged Paulita and hid behind her waiting for the Kid to come back to the house, whereupon they shot him. All accounts agree that the Kid did not recognize Garrett and never fired his gun.

Billy the Kid was buried alongside friends O'Folliard and Bowdre

Chapter 7: Billy the Kid's Life After Death

For decades after the Kid's death, most took Pat Garrett's *The Authentic Life of Billy the Kid* as a factual biography. The book, which was ghostwritten by Ashton Upson, was published in April 1882. Historians have verified that Garrett's book about the Kid is filled with errors, presumably to make the Kid look like a cold-blooded killer and to make Garrett look like the hero that finally stopped him. At the time, Garrett received some heat for the manner in which he killed Billy the Kid, so there's no question he wanted to use his version to portray himself in a more positive light. An updated edition, published in 2000, contains footnotes from historian Frederick Nolan, which help set the record straight.

Nevertheless, the damage done from Garrett's book had deep roots and set the stage for a lot of the mythmaking about the Kid's life. The first edition of the book did not sell well, but by 1954, it was considered a factual reference book. By the 1960s, the book was in libraries in the U.S. and Europe and by the 1970s, the book was in its 10th printing. In an effort to make himself look heroic and to clear his name with those that suggested he unfairly ambushed the Kid, Garrett created one of the greatest legends of the West, even if the legend was based on fiction.

What followed was a slew of dime novels and movies featuring the Kid as the early 20th century equivalent of a bad boy rock star, leaving a trail of dead bodies in his wake. Unlike some icons of the West, the Kid left behind no family to see to it that his story was told correctly, and the lack of solid facts about the Kid's life made it easier to create a legend. If there is no easy way to refute a story, then it lingers as if the possibility remains that it is true.

With such a gap in knowledge, Billy the Kid has plenty of myths to match the legend. One thing that Billy's quotes and his contemporaries' comments suggest is that everyone agreed he was a fairly friendly, witty young man. Regulator Frank Coe later said of him, "I never enjoyed better company. He was humorous and told me many amusing stories. He always found a touch of humor in everything, being naturally full of fun and jollity. Though he was serious in emergencies, his humor was often apparent even in such situations. Billy stood with us to the end, brave and reliable, one of the best soldiers we had. He never pushed in his advice or opinions, but he had a wonderful presence of mind. The tighter the place the more he showed his cool nerve and quick brain. He never seemed to care for money, except to buy cartridges with. Cartridges were scarce, and he always used about ten times as many as everyone else. He would practice shooting at anything he saw, from every conceivable angle, on and off his horse." Frank's cousin George described the Kid as "a brave, resourceful and honest boy. He would have been a successful man under other circumstances. The Kid was a thousand times better and braver than any man hunting him, including Pat Garrett."

Given his legendary ending, like Jesse James, plenty of people came forward in later years claiming that Billy the Kid was not the man killed by Garrett in 1881. One Texan known as Brushy Bill claimed to be the Kid, despite the fact his physical appearance and birth date didn't match the Kid's. Brushy Bill had also once claimed to be part of Jesse James's gang. Not surprisingly, no historian has ever lent credence to Brushy Bill's claims, but Brushy Bill's home town of Hico, Texas opened up the "Billy The Kid Museum" to capitalize off the buzz.

In addition to arguments over how many people the Kid killed, there has been a persistent debate over which hand he shot those people with. Part of the confusion came from the fact that one of the ferrotypes commonly seen was a mirror image of the original. For that reason, Billy the Kid was often believed to be left-handed. Others insist that the Kid was right handed, and Clyde Jeavons, a former curator of the National Film and Television Archive, explained the effect of the ferrotype's mirror image: "You can see by the waistcoat buttons and the belt buckle. This is a common error which has continued to reinforce the myth that Billy the Kid was left-handed. He was not. He was right-handed and carried his gun on his right hip. This particular reproduction error has occurred so often in books and other publications over the years that it has led to the myth that Billy the Kid was left-handed, for which there is no evidence. On the contrary, the evidence (from viewing his photo correctly) is that he was right-handed: he wears his pistol on his right hip with the butt pointing backwards in a conventional right-handed draw position." Ironically, the debate overlooked the fact that the Kid may very well have been ambidextrous: newspaper accounts at the time claimed the Kid shot guns "with his left hand as accurately as he does with his right" and that "his aim with a revolver in each hand, shooting simultaneously, is unerring."

In many ways, the entire state of New Mexico became the Kid's family over time and adopted him as one of its own. Of course, there are financial reasons behind this since Billy the Kid brings in more tourist dollars to the state today than cattle ranching. His only photograph, a 25-cent tintype, was purchased for $2.3 million in a 2011 auction. The image from that tintype can be seen on countless items ranging from mugs to hats to shot glasses at the Kid's own museum in Fort Sumner.

Some New Mexicans have gone so far as to suggest that Billy the Kid should be pardoned for his crimes because Governor Lew Wallace did not keep his end of his bargain with the Kid. Randi McGinn, an attorney from Albuquerque, filed a formal petition for the pardon and set off a debate that raged in New Mexico for seven years. Governor Bill Richardson set up a website to get opinions from the public, although descendants of Pat Garrett and Lew Wallace were clear in their opinion. They were outraged and felt that a pardon was disrespectful to the memories of Garrett and Wallace. In his last day in office on December 31, 2010, Richardson announced on ABC's "Good Morning America" that he gave it serious thought, but that he was not going to pardon the Kid without having a better understanding of why Wallace did not follow through with the pardon.

However, where Billy the Kid really seemed to find his home was among the Mexican-American ranchers in the state who were victimized by the corrupt political system. They were sympathetic to the Kid, partially because they sympathized with his cause, but their acceptance of him was more complex than that. The Mexican-Americans that encountered the Kid embraced him because he embraced them back. The Kid moved easily in the Mexican-American community at a time when many white men would not even consider such a thing. He learned their language, danced their dances, ate their food, and loved their young girls, which may have ultimately led to his demise.

Governor Otero recalled that the Kid was different than other boys his age, obviously affected by being on his own as a child and primarily being in the company of men older than he was. He said that the Kid was bright and eager to learn. Otero was also the first person to try to explain the Kid's special relationship with the Mexican-Americans from the Mexican-American point of view when he published *The Real Billy the Kid: With New Light on the Lincoln County War* in 1936. Otero not only challenged the version of history told from the point of view of the white men, he exposed the level of corruption that the white men brought on the citizens on the county. Historian Frederick Nolan, an acknowledged expert on Billy the Kid, said that there is still much to be learned about the Kid's folk hero status in the Mexican-American culture, but the information will need to come from "that side of the cultural divide." Perhaps that information will shed more light on William Henry McCarty's life, more than just his legend.

Bibliography

Bell, Bob Boze. *The Illustrated Life and Times of Billy the Kid.* Phoenix: Tri-Star Boze Publications. 1992.

Nolan, Frederick. *The West of Billy the Kid.* Norman: University of Oklahoma Press. 1998.

Utley, Robert M. *Billy the Kid: A Short and Violent Life*. Lincoln: University of Nebraska Press. 1989.

Wallis, Michael. *Billy the Kid: Endless Ride.* New York: W.W. Norton & Company. 2007.

Butch Cassidy

Chapter 1: The Early Years of Bob Parker

Robert LeRoy Parker was born in Beaver, Utah on April 13, 1866, just shy of 20 years after Brigham Young led a band of Mormons to Salt Lake City in pursuit of a location to freely practice their religion, far from persecution and scrutiny over their practice of polygamy. Parker was named after his grandfather, an Englishman who led a group of determined Mormon refugees, later known as the Handcart Pioneers, thousands of miles on foot over the Plains, mountainous terrain, and the desert into Utah.

In the late 1850s, that Robert Parker, his wife Ann, and his oldest son, 12 year old Maximilian, walked along the Mormon Trail, pulling all of their belongings in wooden handcarts. Parker was a strong man and a natural leader, making him an obvious choice to take a front position as his group began its journey from Iowa to Utah. However, there was some concern about the weather they would encounter. Leaving Iowa in late August or early September meant the group might very well encounter snow before they reached Salt Lake City, but Parker and the rest of the group put their faith in Brigham Young. He assured them that the Lord would watch over them and keep the snow at bay until they arrived safely.

By mid-October, the pioneers reached the Continental Divide, and, predictably, snow blasted the mountains. Parker led the way and helped break through snowdrifts to clear passage for his family and others, but with a warmer valley in sight, Parker was found dead one morning, still wrapped in his blankets. Young Maximilian dug as deep of a grave as he could in the freezing ground and laid his father to rest before he trudged on toward Utah with the rest of the cold and starving pioneers. When they finally made it to their destination, Max had his first taste of watermelon.

Max and his mother settled at American Fork, about 30 miles south of Salt Lake City. In 1865, they moved to Beaver, and he married Ann Campbell, raising their 13 children in Circleville. Robert, called Bob by most people, was the oldest. When Bob was still a young boy, Max bought a ranch 12 miles south of Circleville, not far from what is now Bryce Canyon National Park. The ranch was known to attract its share of cowboys and cattle rustlers, including an outlaw named Mike Cassidy.

Cassidy, who worked as a cowhand on the ranch, made quite an impression on Bob and taught him some of the most important skills a man of the West could learn, including how to shoot a gun, how to ride a horse, and how to rope, brand, and rustle cattle. For those reasons, contemporaries believed Bob could have had a career as a rancher if he wanted one, and some speculate that he later fronted as a rancher to hide his clandestine, illegal activities. Parker was good with horses and by the time he was 16, he was known as the best shot in Circleville.

Bob grew into a strong, stocky young man, and he was known to be quick-witted and charming. Like Cassidy, he was friendly and jovial much of the time, and just about anyone who encountered him took a liking to him. Not surprisingly, when Butch Cassidy and the Sundance Kid became popular heroes in movies and on television, the two were also turned into a comedic team, needling each other with running dialogue. In one memorable scene from the famous 1969 movie *Butch Cassidy and the Sundance Kid*, Butch says to Sundance, "Is that what you call giving cover?" In response, Sundance retorts, "Is that what you call running?"

Bob's personality is one of the few aspects about his life on which people agree. Indeed, it is not clear when or why Bob developed his disdain for authority and the law. It may have been following an incident between his father and the local Mormon church. The church bishop served as the authority in the community and ruled against Max in a property dispute, leaving the family to have to take odd jobs to try to make ends meet. It may have also been when Bob stole a saddle and was jailed by the sheriff of Garfield County, who some say did not treat the young man well and inadvertently set him on his path toward becoming an outlaw. It can also be safely said that daily interactions with men like Mike Cassidy and outlaws on the ranch had some influence too. Ranching was hard work and it did not take long for Bob to see that there were easier ways to make a living. Mike Cassidy was a hero to Bob, and it is not a stretch to suggest that he heavily influenced him, especially since Parker ended up taking Cassidy's last name as an alias.

At the same time, Bob was never actually a violent man, at least not in the manner that many other Western icons were known to be. He did not hold personal grudges against the lawmen that chased him most of his life, there is no documented evidence that he actually ever killed a man, and he rarely used his gun unless someone shot at him first. In an era where men like Wild Bill Hickok and Doc Holliday allowed exaggerated reports of their kill count so that their reputation preceded them and made them safe, Butch Cassidy did the exact opposite. In fact, Cassidy and the Wild Bunch gang actually tried to downplay their violence and bragged (falsely) that they made every effort to avoid shooting people.

One popular story has Cassidy showing his humanity early on in his career as a criminal when he was arrested for stealing horses near Circleville. According to the legend, Bob did not resist and easily went along with the two men who arrested him. It was a long ride to the county jail and they stopped for lunch when they came across some shade trees near a stream. Bob, who had presented no problems to the deputies but was still handcuffed, watched as one of the men turned toward the stream to dip a bucket in for water. Bob suddenly pushed the officer into the stream. Before the officers realized what was happening, Bob had both of their guns, the handcuff keys, and took off with not only the horses he had already stolen, but their horses, too. He didn't get too far down the trail, though, when he realized that he had all of the canteens. Bob turned around and gave the lawmen the canteens so that they could fill them with water for their walk back to town, telling them that he knew what it was like to be in the desert without water.

Another way that Bob was different from other icons of the West (except perhaps for young Billy the Kid) is that he was never much of a drinker. If he did indulge, he was known to have a taste of "the good stuff" and liked a drink of Mount Vernon whiskey or Old Crow. Those who met him said he was a man of his word. He did like his freedom, though, and he did not like rules. For that reason, Bob knew early that he could not live a life on the straight and narrow path, and he admitted as much to those who urged him to reconsider his ways. His reasons for becoming an outlaw seemed to be tied to his desire to be free from constraints. Bob wanted to make his own rules.

Chapter 2: The Telluride Bank Robbery

Facts about Bob's early life are sketchy, but most historians agree that he worked as a rancher around the West until about 1884, and he seems to have briefly worked as a butcher in Rock

Springs, Wyoming, giving him the nickname, Butch. Whether he took Cassidy as his last name to protect the Parker family name or out of hero worship for Mike Cassidy is not clear, but either way he was known at this time in his life as George "Butch" Cassidy. Over the course of his life, he would have numerous aliases.

For a man destined to become one of the West's most famous outlaws, the first charge brought against Parker was incredibly trivial. In or around 1880, the teenager went to buy clothes and some food from one of the shops in town, but when he arrived he found it was closed. Refusing to leave without what he came for, he took a pair of jeans and pie, and in their place he left an IOU note letting the owner know he would pay for the goods next time he came to the shop. In response, the shopkeeper filed a charge against the kid. A jury later acquitted him.

Telluride is on the western slopes of the San Juan Mountains in southwestern Colorado, and when Cassidy arrived in 1889, it was a wild mining town filled with prospectors lured by the dream of finding gold in the nearby hills. As was the case with all mining towns, whiskey flowed easily in Telluride, and men looked to the gambling halls, saloons, and brothels to blow off steam. Furthermore, the San Miguel Valley Bank was a tempting lure to potential bank robbers. The small wooden building did not look like much from the outside, but in an attempt to impress investors, the interior was lavishly decorated. Years later, Matt Warner said, "I didn't know before that there was any place in the world with such rich trimmings and furnishings as the inside of that bank."[20] Naturally, that same interior impressed those looking to withdraw money from the bank too, especially those who didn't have an account there.

Warner met Cassidy somewhere along the way before the scheme to rob the San Miguel bank was devised. The two men partnered on the ownership of a race horse named Betty and stole livestock, among other things. In the days leading up to the robbery, Warner, Cassidy, and Tom McCarty were seen freely spending money around town, giving no signs of being men in need of cash. Speculation is that the money they were spending came courtesy of a robbery in Denver, but they also spent money intentionally as part of their plan. According to Warner, they wanted to seem like they were in town to have a good time, not to case the local bank.

The morning of June 24, 1889, four men checked their horses out of the local livery and patronized the saloons near the San Miguel Valley Bank. At noon, bank employee Charlie Painter left the bank, leaving only one teller remaining on duty. Two of the four robbers waited outside of the bank with the horses and the other two robbers went inside. One of the bandits told the teller that he wanted to cash a check and when the teller took a closer look, the bandit shoved his face into the desk and told him to keep quiet. The other three robbers entered the bank and scooped up all of the money they could find. For unknown reasons, they did not wear masks or try to shield their identity. Exact accounts of the robbery and Cassidy's role vary, but within

---

[20] Patterson, Richard. *Butch Cassidy: A Biography.* Page 21.

minutes, the men took off with over $20,000. In addition to McCarty, Warner, and Cassidy, the fourth man has been speculated to be any number of outlaws, including Harry Longabaugh (the Sundance Kid) and Dan Parker, Butch Cassidy's brother. It may also have been one of McCarty's brothers.

On their way out of town, the robbers crossed paths with two other men from town. The men recognized Warner and Cassidy, a mistake that Warner claims set them on their path as outlaws for good because it made sure that they were always on the run. Warner also said that McCarty commented after they continued down the trail that he should have shot the two men.

Chapter 3: Wyoming State Penitentiary

After the Telluride robbery, it is believed that Cassidy and his fellow outlaws hid out at Robbers Roost in southeastern Utah. The remote area made it an ideal hiding place for outlaws because it was difficult to get to and easy to defend if a lawman was so bold as to approach. As it would turn out, no members of law enforcement even knew of its existence until after Cassidy's death. Given that Cassidy and his gang built cabins there and stored cattle, horses, and assorted weaponry, it is safe to assume that Robbers Roost was used frequently, and that the outlaws may have even used the area during winters. The area was made famous again a century later when hiker Aron Ralston amputated his own arm to free himself from an 800-pound boulder. His story was the subject of the 2011 movie, *127 Hours*.

In 1890, Cassidy bought a ranch near Dubois, Wyoming, and in 1894, he began a sporadic relationship with a teenage girl named Ann Bassett, the daughter of a local and prominent cattle rancher named Herb Bassett. Ann's sister, Josie, was also known to have a relationship with another of Cassidy's associates and future member of the Wild Bunch, Elzy Lay. Ann and Josie were considered to be intelligent women who also knew the ranching business. Their father did business with Cassidy, and it is speculated that part of the motivation for the sisters to have romantic relationships with Cassidy and Lay, as well as other Cassidy associates, was to keep other outlaws from harassing them. Women were rarely allowed to visit the hideout at Robbers Roost, but Ann and Josie were two of the ones that spent time there.

Ann Bassett

Elzy Lay

The other famous hideout for Cassidy and his gang, which came to be known as the Wild Bunch, was Hole-in-the-Wall north of Casper, Wyoming. It was ideal for ranchers thanks to the open grazing land, but the remote location and one-way entry also made it a good hideout. In addition, Cassidy's gang spent time at Brown's Hole, a canyon located near the Green River, where the borders of Utah, Wyoming, and Colorado meet.

The site of Hole-in-the-Wall

Cassidy, for the only time in his life, found himself behind bars in 1894. Whether he was living the life of a law-abiding citizen or he simply had not been caught, he had managed to stay out of trouble with the law for nearly four years, but he was eventually arrested for stealing horses. He may have been arrested and released for insufficient evidence prior to this, but this time he was taken to Lander, Wyoming for a trial and convicted. Cassidy was sentenced to two years in the Wyoming State Penitentiary in Laramie. Legend has it that Cassidy asked the local sheriff if he could leave for the night, promising to return the next morning to serve his prison sentence. Even more incredibly, the sheriff not only agreed but even let Cassidy use his horse. Legend had it that Cassidy used the opportunity to say farewell to Ann Bassett before serving his time. If the story is true, Cassidy must have kept his word because he was certainly a prisoner in the Wyoming State Penitentiary.

Cassidy, whose occupation was listed as "cowboy" in his prison file, was on his best behavior in prison. He petitioned Wyoming Governor William Richards for an early release, and Richards reportedly agreed to let him go if Cassidy would stay out of trouble in Wyoming. Cassidy was released from prison on January 19, 1896 and from there, he promptly went to either Hole-in-the-Wall or Brown's Hole.

Joined by the likes of George "Flat Nose" Curry and the Sundance Kid, the core of the Wild Bunch began to take shape. However, much that has been written about the Wild Bunch is myth. In fact, it was not until the Pinkerton Detective Agency called them the Wild Bunch that anyone had ever heard the name. As many as 30 different men have been linked to the gang at various times, but very few of them committed more than one or two holdups with each other. It's also unclear how many crimes they were actually responsible for and just how many Butch Cassidy and Sundance Kid actively participated in. Only three heists can be linked back to them, but their reputation was firmly established, and Cassidy and Sundance were soon two of the most wanted men in both North and South America.

Sitting (L-R): Harry A. Longabaugh (The Sundance Kid), Ben Kilpatrick (The Tall Texan), and Butch Cassidy
Standing (L-R): Will Carver (News Carver), and Harvey Logan (Kid Curry)

Chapter 4: The Wild Bunch on the Loose

Montpelier, Idaho

The majority of the crimes the Wild Bunch committed occurred between 1896 and 1901, and it was during this time that they moved on from horse theft, which can be cumbersome, to robbing banks and railroads. Banks were especially worth the effort to the gang because they were sure to have money and the timing was easier to predict.

The first bank that Cassidy is believed to have robbed as a member of the Wild Bunch was in Montpelier, Idaho on a hot summer day on August 13, 1896. A local storekeeper saw three men walking their horses along a street around 3:00 p.m., and he watched as they got back on their horses, rode over to the bank, and dismounted. Two men standing on the sidewalk gave them a quick glance, but thought nothing of their appearance until two of the strangers pulled their bandanas over the faces and pointed revolvers at them. The robbers forced the two men inside and lined them up facing a wall with numerous customers and two of the three bank employees on duty. The assistant cashier was told to stay in place.

A man assumed to be Cassidy kept his gun pointed at the frightened people while his partner, a taller man that is believed to have been Lay, relieved the bank of all its cash, gold, and silver, totaling over $7,000. When he had it all, he loaded the bags onto a pack mule and a horse. Cassidy advised the people inside to bank to wait at least 10 minutes before alerting authorities and calmly walked out the door and got on his horse. The three bandits then took off for the edge of town.

When he was sure that they were gone, the cashier ran over to the sheriff's office to tell the deputy what had happened. Though the deputy had neither a gun nor a horse and was mainly a process server, not a lawman, he was not willing to simply let the bandits get away without a chase. Thus, he hopped on a bike and headed out after the robbers. The chase was futile, but he did note that they had headed east, toward Wyoming. The only robber of the three that did not wear a mask was Bob Meeks, who did not want to attract attention while he was standing outside on the street. However, this allowed the cashier to get a good look at him, and Meeks was the only one of the three that was caught and eventually convicted of the crime.

Castle Gate, Utah

Cassidy usually did not like to rob banks or trains in Utah for fear of being recognized, but he made an exception for the Pleasant Valley Coal Company in Castle Gate and masterminded what many consider to be one of the most bold and daring crimes in American history. When it was over, he was famous on both sides of the law.

The Castle Gate mine was the largest coalmine in Carbon County, Utah. Its location in Price also made it ideal for Cassidy because it was between Robbers Roost and Brown's Hole. The large payroll that a mine of this size required made the company nervous, and the risk of outlaws lying in wait for the payroll to arrive on a scheduled train was far too great. Thus, the company had irregular paydays and tried to keep irregular schedules. Cassidy studied the train and decided that robbing the train itself was too risky, ultimately concluding that the gang would have to make their move against the paymaster.

However, without knowing exactly when the payroll would arrive, that plan required some patience. In mid-April 1897, Cassidy rode into town and asked a local barkeep if there was any work available for a rancher. He was told there might be if he waited around long enough. Cassidy thanked the man for the information and rode over to the train depot. His mare, unfamiliar with the sound of the train whistle, nearly bucked Cassidy out of his saddle. After the train departed, Cassidy went back to the saloon and worked his way through some Old Crow.

Every day for a week, Cassidy repeated the scene with every train that came into town, and his horse eventually got used to the noise from the train. On April 21, 1897 at 12:40 p.m., the train he was waiting for rolled into town. A whistle blasted to alert the miners that today would be payday, or so they thought. Cassidy saw the paymaster, E.L. Carpenter, and two assistants carry moneybags toward Carpenter's office. Carpenter was walking gingerly due to a sore toe.

Each man came out with a heavy bag. One had $700 in gold, one had $7,000 in gold, and the third had $100 in silver. As the men approached the stairs that led to their office, Carpenter felt the butt of Cassidy's revolver in his ribs. Cassidy smiled and told Carpenter that he would take the money bags and would hate to have to shoot him if he didn't comply. For a moment, Carpenter could not believe he was being robbed. Miners were everywhere, but most did not speak English and probably had no idea what was happening.

Carpenter dropped his bags and his assistant dropped the bag of silver and hid in the nearby hardware store. It occurred to Carpenter that he had seen Cassidy and one of the other men (likely Lay) earlier in the week. He noticed the horses, too, and realized that should have tipped him off. Horses were not a common sight in mining towns because the trails were too steep.

Cassidy handed Lay some of the money and got ready to mount his own horse and take off out of town, but before they did Carpenter yelled out that he had been robbed. In the chaos, Cassidy's horse got spooked and ran off, leaving Cassidy holding a bag of stolen gold with no means for a getaway. Lay was able to track the horse down, with Cassidy trailing behind on foot. Somehow, Cassidy got back on the horse, gold still in hand, and the bandits headed out of town with over $7,000. They left the bag of silver behind.

Carpenter ran for the telegraph office to alert the authorities 10 miles away in Price. However, the telegraph operator told him there was no signal because the lines had been cut. Carpenter then went to the train and told the engineer to head for Price. He didn't realize as the train steamed along the tracks that they passed Cassidy and Lay along the way.

When Carpenter got to Price, he told the sheriff what had happened, but it took several hours before the sheriff could organize a posse. Carpenter went to the telegraph office in Price to alert the other towns in the area about the presence of the bandits, but another member of the Wild Bunch, Joe Walker, had cut the telegraph wires leading out of the canyon.

A posse led by Joe Bush gave Cassidy and Lay a good chase across Utah, but Cassidy had the advantage. In addition to having planned the robbery for months, he was on his home turf. It didn't hurt that Cassidy was generous with the price he paid for fresh horses when he came across a rancher that would let him switch out his mounts. The locals felt no loyalty to the mining company and were happy to oblige the outlaws. When they had made it 70 miles across the desert to San Rafael, Cassidy and Lay met Joe Walker and split up the stolen gold coins.

Cassidy, Lay, and Walker went to Robbers Roost to hide out while the chaos died down, and the gang passed the time by gambling, drinking, racing horses, and telling stories. Ann Bassett was there with two other women, and the girls were particularly useful when the camp ran out of supplies. It was no secret to the lawmen in Utah that Cassidy and his gang were hiding out in the Robbers Roost area, but none made any attempt to ride in there. Local newspapers suggested that the sheriffs and deputies were afraid to try.

After three months of waiting, the outlaws had all they could take and decided it was time to spend some of their money. In June 1897, they went back to Brown's Hole, gathered some friends, and headed toward their favorite saloons in Wyoming. Some of the money was spent on shaves, haircuts, and new clothes. Guns were shot all in the name of fun and the bandits paid the saloonkeepers at a rate of one dollar per hole for repairs.

The Union Pacific Train Robberies

Cassidy is often linked to a spectacular train robbery in Wilcox, Wyoming on June 2, 1899. Two men flagged a Union Pacific train down, and, thinking that the strangers might be alerting the engineer that a bridge was out, the train screeched to a stop. The men got away with about $50,000 in gold and thousands more in personal effects, and they also blew up the tracks and blasted open the safe with sticks of dynamite, sending paper money floating into the sky. In a shootout following the robbery, Sheriff Joe Hazen was killed, likely shot by Kid Curry and Flatnose Curry.

Harvey Logan (Kid Curry)

There is no evidence linking Cassidy to the train robbery in Wyoming, and it's plausible that he was not there. After all, he may have been keeping his word to the state's governor that he would commit no more crimes in Wyoming in exchange for early release from prison. But even if he wasn't there, the death of Sheriff Hazen implicated the Wild Bunch, and the crime got the Pinkerton Detective Agency involved. In fact, it was Pinkerton's famous detective agency that labeled Cassidy's gang the Wild Bunch, and the Pinkertons had their sights set on Cassidy and the Wild Bunch for the next decade. It was their dogged pursuit of the gang that would eventually induce Cassidy and Sundance to flee the country.

The Pinkerton agency collected the most detailed data on the movements of Cassidy, Sundance, and their female companion going by the name of Etta Place, and they knew more about the Wild Bunch than any other agency or law enforcement department. There are some who believe that Etta, who the Pinkertons called Ethel, was actually Ann Basset, but this was never confirmed. Although the pictures of Etta and Ann look strikingly alike, authorities strongly believe that Etta Place was with Sundance in South America from 1902-1904, while Ann was arrested for rustling cattle in Utah in 1903.

The name and fate of Etta Place has remained one of the most enduring mysteries of the Butch and Sundance legend, and aside from the fact she was a long-time companion of Sundance's, little else is known about her. Whoever she was, Etta Place was using the maiden name of

Sundance's mother (Annie Place), and she was referred to at times as Mrs. Harry Longabaugh or Mrs. Harry A. Place. She also once signed her name "Mrs. Ethel Place". Assuming she wasn't Ann Bassett, Etta Place was only one of five known women allowed in Robbers Roost, including the Bassett sisters, Elzy Lay's girlfriend Maude Davis, and gang member Laura Bullion.

The Pinkerton Agency's mugshot of Laura Bullion

With operatives spread across both North and South America, the Pinkertons had the ability to track Cassidy and the Wild Bunch when the trail went cold for law enforcement. Charlie Siringo, working under the alias Charles L. Carter on behalf of the Pinkertons, managed to infiltrate the

Wild Bunch after the Wilcox robbery. Information obtained by Siringo put the heat on several members of the Wild Bunch, resulting in the capture of Kid Curry, who was killed in a shootout in Colorado in 1904. Though not the most notorious of the gang, Kid Curry was the most feared, and it is believed he killed nearly 10 law enforcement officers in his short life. After he was captured in Tennessee, he headed to Montana and murdered a rancher who he claimed killed his brother years earlier. He was captured in Tennessee and escaped a second time, only to finally be killed in the Colorado shootout.

There were other robberies attributed to the Wild Bunch, including a Union Pacific train in Tipton, Wyoming and a Great Northern train in Malta, Montana that netted $45,000. On September 19, 1900, Cassidy and Sundance may have been involved in a bank robbery in Winnemucca, Nevada. It is extremely difficult, if not impossible, to know just which, if any, of the Wild Bunch crimes during their five-year heyday can be directly attributed to Cassidy. Nearly everyone who has researched his past agrees that it was not his style to harm innocent people, so any suggestion of him participating in violent crimes are subject to further questioning. Regardless of which crimes were linked to him, he was on the radar of the Pinkertons.

An Attempt at Amnesty

In many ways, Cassidy proved himself to be cut from a different mold than other outlaws. He was a congenial man who had many friends who were not outlaws. During times when he was on the run, he was able to mix and mingle with relative ease among the law-abiding locals. Wherever he went, whether it was his ranch in Dubois or his ranch in Argentina, he got along with his neighbors and was respected as a hard-working man. If he did not want to live the fugitive's life, it would come as no surprise.

In 1899, Cassidy visited the office of attorney Orlando Powers in Ogden, Utah. The two men did not know each other, but they knew of each other from when Cassidy financed the defense of Matt Warner, E.B. Coleman, and Dave Wall. The men had been charged with murder in a mining claim dispute in Vernal, Utah, and the money used for their defense most likely came from the bank robbery in Montpelier.

Cassidy laid out his case for Powers. He explained that he was being portrayed as a vicious outlaw and had been given a reputation that was different from reality. He told Powers that he had never committed murder and only robbed banks and trains, not people. He appealed to Powers, who he buttered up by calling him the best lawyer in Utah, to make an arrangement with the governor to grant Cassidy amnesty or perhaps allow him to plead guilty to lesser charges. If he could get a deal like that, Cassidy said, he would go straight and leave his life of crime behind.

Powers reportedly said that it was unlikely that such a deal could be granted. Cassidy was wanted for too many crimes by large companies, and even if Cassidy claimed that there were no witnesses who could be used against him in court, those companies would have found someone. He advised Cassidy that his best bet was to go back in hiding.

Cassidy did not stop with Powers, however. His next visit was to Parley P. Christensen, an attorney in Salt Lake City. Christensen, a graduate of Cornell University School of Law and one of the brightest young politicians in the Republican Party, knew Governor Heber Wells. They were both delegates at the state constitutional convention in 1895 and Christensen later served on the Utah legislature. Cassidy hoped that Christensen's personal connection with Wells would boost his chances at getting a deal.

Christensen

After meeting with Christensen, Cassidy had some hope. Wells agreed to a meeting with Cassidy, and after hearing his proposal Wells said that if there were no murder warrants against him, they could work out a deal. Cassidy, sure that there would be no such warrants, was confident that a deal would be made, but when Utah's district attorney checked Cassidy's record, he did find his name on a murder warrant. At Cassidy's second meeting with the governor, he told him about the warrant and said that he would not be able to make a deal. Cassidy was incredulous and insisted that he never killed a man, but Wells explained that all that was needed was for his name to appear on a warrant. With all of the bank and train robberies that were occurring, the Wild Bunch was usually considered the top band of suspects. On top of that, it would have been easy for Cassidy's name to surface anytime other members of the Wild Bunch pulled a job and killed someone in the aftermath. If someone said they say Butch Cassidy was on the scene or suspected him of being there, his name could easily be on a warrant.

Governor Wells

It was at this point that Powers had another idea for Cassidy. He proposed the idea of Cassidy not only agreeing to stop living a life of crime but work as an express guard for the Union Pacific Railroad. If he agreed to this, perhaps Union Pacific would agree to drop their charges against him. Powers felt that this would allow the railroad to keep close tabs on Cassidy, as well as possibly serve as a deterrent against further attacks if other bandits knew he was on the train.

Despite the fact that such an arrangement would do nothing to eliminate the charges against Cassidy from other railroad lines or from the growing list of states in which he was wanted, there is evidence to suggest that Cassidy may have accepted the deal. A letter dated May 30, 1900 addressed to Governor Wells was located in the governor's collection of papers in the Utah State Archives. The letter was from W.S. Seavey, an agent for the Thiel Detective Service's Denver office and the former chief of police for the Omaha Police Department. Seavey said, "I desire to inform you that I have reliable information to the effect that if the authorities will let him alone and the UPRR officials will give him a job as guard, etc., the outlaw Butch Cassidy will lay down his arms, come in, give himself up, go to work and be a good peacable [sic] citizen hereafter."[21]

For reasons that are not clear, the deal never happened. For many years, rumors persisted that the Union Pacific officials stood Cassidy up, prompting him to write a note telling the railroad executives what they could do with their deal. However, historians have determined that no such note likely ever existed. It is more likely that if such as deal was under consideration, the railroad understood that it presented too much risk and not enough reward for them. They had long viewed Harvey Logan (Kid Curry) as far more dangerous than Butch Cassidy, and they might rightly have wondered how Cassidy would have been able to hold Logan or any other member of the Wild Bunch off if they tried to rob one of their trains. There would also have obviously been questions about whether or not Cassidy could be trusted to not divulge the details of payroll trains to his associates. Certainly the railroad's board of directors, who had paid $110 million to buy the company in 1893, would have had reservations about letting one of the West's most notorious outlaws guard their investment.

Chapter 5: South America

At this stage in the game, Cassidy no doubt sensed that the odds against him either staying out of a jail cell or simply staying alive were stacking up against him. He had built up enough cash to make a new start in South America and, with only Sundance willing to go with him, the two men split up before reconnecting on February 1, 1902. The meeting place was New York City.

Sundance showed up in New York with Etta Place, which gives credence to the likelihood that Cassidy had every intention of leaving crime behind. Had he planned to resume his thieving ways, he likely would not have consented to the presence of a woman. The trio stayed at Miss Taylor's boarding house on West Twelfth Street, with Cassidy signing the register under the name Jim Ryan and the other two claiming to be Mr. and Mrs. Harry Place. Soon after that, Sundance visited Tiffany's and bought a new lapel pin for himself and a watch for Etta. From there, they had their portrait taken at DeYoung's studio on Broadway, looking for all the world like a pair of the most refined citizens in New York.

---

[21] Patterson, Richard. "Butch Cassidy's Surrender Offer." *True West Magazine,* June 12, 2006.

The DeYoung portrait of Sundance and Etta Place, whose identity remains a mystery

After three weeks in New York, they boarded the S.S. Soldier Prince, bound for Buenos Aires, Argentina. Shortly after their arrival, Sundance deposited $12,000 in the London and Platte River Bank, permitting them to apply for land. The application was approved, and they reached their land holdings in Cholilo in May. Their closest neighbor was a dentist, and they wasted no time in giving all appearances that they intended to be law-abiding ranchers.

However, the Pinkerton agency had not given up the pursuit and was able to trace the trio to Buenos Aires. On July 1, 1903, Robert Pinkerton wrote to the chief of police in Buenos Aires and included the most recent photographs and descriptions of the fugitives. A local operative was asked to visit the ranch and make an arrest, but some say he declined because it was the rainy season and travel inland was too difficult. In the meantime, the police chief agreed to monitor their movements in the event that they tried to leave the country.

Whatever the circumstances, Cassidy, Sundance, and Etta lived a life of relative peace until the spring of 1906. It is not clear if they heard that the Pinkertons were going to make a move or if they simply got the urge to resume their criminal ways, but with Etta calmly holding the horses, an American fugitive helped Cassidy and Sundance rob a bank in Mercedes of $20,000. One of the three men killed the banker in the process. They split the proceeds and went their separate ways. Cassidy and Sundance were on the run again.

That robbery set off reports that they were involved in robberies throughout South America, including banks at Bahia Blanca and in Rio Gallegos and a payroll train at Eucalyptus. They were even accused of killing a man in Arroyo Pescado in 1910, but this seems unlikely because murder was not their style and, more importantly, it is highly likely that they were dead by then.

What became of Etta Place is a mystery. The last written record of her is at Arroyo Pescado and then she disappeared from sight, despite the fact that the Pinkerton agency was supposedly keeping close tabs on her. Of course, there were also many in law enforcement that had given up on the idea of catching Cassidy and Sundance as well, since they always seemed to be a step ahead of the people that were chasing them.

Early in 1909, the payroll for the Aramayo mines, located in the southern region of Bolivia, was robbed. That is a fact, but what happened after that is up for debate. Most historians agree that Cassidy and Sundance made their way to San Vicente on November 6. The local justice, known as the corregidor, made arrangements for them to stay in a spare room at the home of a local villager. Some say that it was a mule that gave them away to the corregidor. Cassidy and Sundance had taken the equipment off of their horses and mules, setting it all aside and letting the animals graze. Supposedly, the corregidor watched one of the mules roll on its back in the dust and recognized it as an animal that belonged to his friend. The mule had been used to transport the payroll to the Aramayo mines. He was suspicious, but also found the casual manner of Cassidy and Sundance to be unusual if they were, indeed, responsible for the robbery.

He alerted four members of the Bolivian cavalry, including a captain, that the Aramayo mine bandits may be in town. Soon after that, one of the soldiers entered a room where Cassidy and Sundance were staying – some say that they were fueling up on food and whiskey – but he was met by Cassidy, who shot and killed him. If true, this is believed to be the only man Cassidy ever killed. The other two men took cover and fired into the room. In the mean time, the captain instructed the corregidor to round up men from the village to surround the building to keep

Cassidy and Sundance from escaping.

There are different versions of what may have happened next. There are reports that Sundance ran out onto the patio, shooting as he went, hoping to reach the rifles that were leaning along a wall. He was shot before he reached the end of the courtyard. Cassidy ran out to get him, taking more than one bullet himself, and dragged the mortally wounded Sundance back inside. There are also reports that shortly after the captain arrived, three loud screams were heard coming from the building, followed by silence.

The Bolivian army reported that when they finally entered the room they found the men believed to be Butch and Sundance dead. Sundance's body had several gunshot wounds to the arms and one to the forehead, while Cassidy had a wound to an arm and had also been shot in the temple. The Bolivians concluded that Cassidy put Sundance out of his misery before turning the gun on himself because they were out of ammunition. However, there are also reports that they had plenty of ammunition and Sundance even had a rifle nearby. The outlaws did have the money from the Aramayo mine, as well as map of Bolivia, and the payroll officer confirmed that the dead men were the same men that committed the robbery. An inquest was held, but Bolivian officials never officially identified the names of the dead bandits, who were quickly buried in the San Vicente cemetery.

Chapter 6: Dead or Alive?

Reports soon got back to friends of Cassidy and Sundance in Bolivia that they had died in San Vicente. The last reported sighting of them was at the Hotel Terminus in Tupiza. A friend greeted Cassidy as Mr. Maxwell, one of his aliases, but Cassidy reportedly said that he was now going by Santiago Lowe. A man by that name was, indeed, a guest of the hotel that night. When mail sent to Sundance in 1909 was unanswered, attempts were made to settle his estate in Chile. Death certificates were forwarded for the bandits killed in San Vicente, but their names were listed as "unknown." None of the newspaper articles about the incident ever referred to the outlaws by name, nor did they speculate that the famous Butch Cassidy and Sundance Kid had met their demise in the gun battle.

It was not until a wire service story out of Argentina suggested that the two unnamed bandits were the same men who robbed a bank in Mercedes that the Cassidy/Sundance connection was made. The first English account of the shootout in San Vicente came in "Across South America," a 1911 travelogue by Hiram Bingham. In 1913, A.G. Francis wrote "The End of an Outlaw" for *World Wide Magazine* and discussed his encounters with Cassidy and who he identified as Kid Curry, rather than Sundance. Some of the information was accurate, but the Pinkerton agency declared that the article was fiction. Books followed in 1922 and 1924 that discussed the shootout in San Vicente, but details were still vague.

In 1930, a friend of Cassidy, Percy Seiber, granted an interview to Arthur Chapman for an article for *The Elks Magazine*. Seiber gave Chapman a glorified account of the shootout. It is believed he is the first one to suggest that Cassidy and Sundance faced an army of Bolivian soldiers rather than four men and some villagers as back-up. He also put Cassidy and Sundance at crimes that they could not possibly have committed. Still, historians referred to the article as fact for years. When William Goldman wrote the screenplay for the 1969 movie *Butch Cassidy and the Sundance Kid*, he used two books as reference material that incorporated the fabrications from Seiber.

After Chapman's article, the legend of Butch Cassidy and the Sundance Kid grew, fueled largely by fascination with the Wild West. An engaging character in reality, Butch Cassidy naturally made great fodder for western fiction. Despite the fact that they had committed a grand total of two robberies in the eight years that they lived in South America, they were portrayed as bandits responsible for an array of heists, holdups, and robberies. The 1969 movie, starring two of the biggest box office stars of the time, Paul Newman and Robert Redford, also rekindled interest in the men in the 1970s.

However, now the story shifted away from the notion that they died in Bolivia, but that they had planted the story so that they could escape to any number of places to live in obscurity. Mexico, Ireland, France, Arizona, Georgia, Idaho, and Washington are just some of the mentioned possibilities. Just as there are those who claim to see Elvis Presley in just about any location that can be imagined, so were there a plethora of Butch Cassidy sightings.

Unfortunately, several attempts to write about the fate of Cassidy were not simply speculation and theories but poorly researched books and articles that were unsupported by any sort of fact. One particularly unusual theory was made by Ed Kirby, a self-proclaimed expert on Butch Cassidy, who wrote a book claiming that the Sundance Kid died a homeless man in a Utah penitentiary going by the alias Hiram BeBee. When confronted with the fact BeBee was nine inches shorter than Sundance, Kirby attributed it to osteoporosis.

That there really are no concrete facts about the shootout in San Vicente makes it easier to accept that Cassidy and Sundance did not die in Bolivia. One person who fueled the fire on the idea that Cassidy, at least, returned to the U.S. is his sister, Lula Parker Betenson. Her brother left the family home in Utah when Lula was a baby. She wrote a book in 1975 that chronicled the life of her family and her famous brother's exploits, including the claim that he returned to visit the family in 1925. Lula never did reveal the alias that her brother was using, but she did say that he lived in Spokane, Washington, although he was not the same man in Spokane who got his 15 minutes of fame by stating he was the "real" Butch Cassidy.

Understandably, her claim caught the attention of historians, who visited with Lula to get more information but came away with the impression that Lula knew very little about Cassidy. One of her sons simply said that she made up the fact that he had visited in 1925. Later, Lula said that she was just having some fun with the stories. What is probably most important is that if Cassidy was still alive, he never visited his father, who lived to be 94 years old and spent a considerable amount of time searching for his son when it was not clear what had happened to him. However, Cassidy could have been aware that the Pinkerton agency would have likely found out if he reached out to his father.

Regardless of when he actually died, like many Western icons the legend of Butch Cassidy has lived on in popular culture. The irony is that he is eternally associated with Longabaugh, the Sundance Kid, despite the fact Cassidy was actually far better friends with Elzy Lay and almost certainly did more jobs with him. Lay had been captured in Carlsbad, New Mexico in 1899 and sentenced to life in the New Mexico State Penitentiary, but Governor Miguel Otero pardoned him in 1906 for assisting in getting the prison warden's wife and daughter released when inmates took them hostage. Lay retired from crime after that. The imprisonment of Lay had a tremendous impact on Cassidy, and some suggest it had much to do with his desire to go straight.

One of Cassidy's first appearances as a film character was in the 1951 movie *The Texas Rangers*, in which Cassidy is played by John Doucette and the Sundance Kid is portrayed by Ian McDonald. Five years later, Cassidy and Sundance were in *The Three Outlaws*, and Sundance was played by Alan Hale, Jr., who went on to fame in the role of the Skipper in the 1960s comedy *Gilligan's Island*. In 1965, Arthur Hunnicut played Cassidy in the Western comedy *Cat Ballou*. The idea that Cassidy lived on was also portrayed in film in 2011. Sam Shepherd played Cassidy in *Blackthorn*, a movie about Cassidy living out his life as James Blackthorn in a secluded Bolivian village.

Still, the most famous of all of the movies to portray Cassidy was the 1969 film *Butch Cassidy and the Sundance Kid*. Goldman took eight years to write the script and later said that they couldn't find any actors to play the parts, which is ironic given how the movie became part of classic cinema. In 2003, it was selected by the Library of Congress to be part of a group of films preserved by the National Film Registry due to its cultural significance. Goldman recalled years later that he wanted to show how these were different outlaws than audiences were used to and that this story was not like other westerns. Goldman even had a difficult time selling the idea of Cassidy and Sundance running away to South America. Movie executives said that audiences would not buy it, despite the fact that it actually happened. The film was a box office smash and was nominated for numerous Academy Awards, with Goldman winning the Oscar for Best Screenplay.

The fascination with Butch Cassidy in popular culture is not difficult to understand. He was one of the last of the notorious Western outlaws to die "with his boots on", living in a time of rapid change in American society. Even the 1969 movie pays homage to this with a scene in which Cassidy and Sundance express dismay at the cold, impersonal nature of banks. Of course, these banks were also catching up to the likes of the Wild Bunch with technology, making the life of bank robbers that much more challenging.

Despite his place in pop culture and the glorification of men like him, the simplest definition of Cassidy is that he was a criminal. However, the glimpses of his character that come through in stories about his life show a man more complex than that. Perhaps this is why, a century later, Butch Cassidy is a household name and movies are still made about him. If there is any character that Americans gravitate to the most, it's the character of a person living by his or her own rules. Cassidy tried to do that within the constraints of life as a criminal on the run. If he did not die in the shootout in Bolivia, perhaps he was finally able to get what he had searched for his entire life and was, at last, truly able to live his life on his own terms.

Bibliography

Kelly, Charles. The Outlaw Trail: A History of Butch Cassidy and his Wild Bunch. Lincoln, NE: University of Nebraska Press. 1996 (reprinted edition).

Patterson, Richard. "Butch Cassidy's Surrender Offer." *True West Magazine*. June 12, 2006.

Patterson, Richard. Butch Cassidy: A Biography. Lincoln, NE: University of Nebraska Press. 1998.

Rutter, Michael. Outlaw Tails of Utah: True Stories of Utah's Most Famous Rustlers, Robbers, and Bandits. Guilford, CT: Globe Pequot Press.

Printed in Great Britain
by Amazon.co.uk, Ltd.,
Marston Gate.